I0086290

Are You Enslaved by Your Emotions?

Rozália Horváth Balázsi

SYDNEY AUSTRALIA

Are You Enslaved by Your Emotions?

ISBN 978-0-646-54514-1

Edited by Margaret Tucker

Illustrated ad typesetting by Virginia Smith

If you wish to contact the author:

Ph: +61 2 9521 3951

Australia Sydney NSW

Email: rozalia1@optusnet.com.au

Web: http://www.akashicrecords-tarot.com

Author's Biography

Rozália is a Clairvoyant and Conscious Channel from the Akashic Records. She was born in Hungary, and from 1968 she has lived in Sydney Australia.

Rozália is descended from a long line of distinguished Spiritual clairvoyants. For many years she has been teaching in the field of Esoteric Metaphysical Self Awareness. The subjects include: meditation, crystals, chakra balancing, aura and color reading, basic astrology, tarot cards, palm reading, spiritual healing and how to learn to channel and work with the Ascended Masters and their Governing Hierarchy. She is well known and respected in the field of physic divination when reading Palms, Tarot or karmic relationships with astrology.

When I self-published my first book "*How to Channel from the Akashic Records*", I received a large amount of feedback about how much my book has helped so many people. Nevertheless, I also received feedback from a small number of people, who purchased the Tarot book, and informed me that they were not interested in learning how to read the Tarot, but when they read the chapter titled: "*the Meta Physical information guidelines and principles*," they found that it was unique and interesting. They realized that those Meta Physical principals do not just apply to the tarot cards, but any spiritually inclined work falls under these "*traffic rules*." The next thing I needed to do regarding this information was to request in my next meditation a meeting with my Spiritual Hierarchy. They then gave me their blessing to write another book and set the platform for the Souls Journey and the hardship of the emotional body and its every day realities.

Once again I received new information which I had not been aware of to this extent. I am referring to **homosexual people** and the purpose they serve in our evolutionary cycle. Once you read this book you will not have any more excuses not to change your life for the better.
Because the truth will set you free.

Contents

1st Chapter; The Realm of the 24 Elders and its Hierarchies..........**7**

2nd Chapter; The Family Tree of the Over Souls and its Egoes....**21**

3rd Chapter; The Soul Consciousness is Ready to be Reborn.......**37**

4th Chapter; The Human Aura and the Seven Major Chakras.......**49**

5th Chapter; The Three Genders & Three Major Life Forces **73**

6th Chapter; Three Levels of Consciousness within the Mind......**87**

7th Chapter; Personal and Family Karma....................................**107**

8th Chapter; The Martyr's Pathways **117**

9th Chapter; Meditations, Mantras and Prayers..........................**125**

10th Chapter; Crystals to Aid and Protect You **145**

Preface

According to ancient Mayan prophecies, throughout the period approaching 2012, this cycle of evolution (the third dimensional way of life) is about to end and move into the fifth dimension which represents a conscious awareness of the Spirit. So what does this really mean to us all? The answers are many, as the questions arise. For the benefit of those who just happened to step onto the road of self-discovery, in order to understand what taking place is right now, how those changes are going to affect us, and how we fit into the scheme of things, we have to start from the beginning.

In this book, I will attempt to shed some clarity and understanding regarding the following questions: do we have any reason to be alive? Or are we nothing more than just a fluke of nature? Is there anyone out there who is running our lives and calling the shots? On the other hand, have you ever asked yourself why some people can get away with blue murder, and others cannot? The first time you think about those questions, I am afraid the magic solution will not appear instantly on a silver platter for you.

However, what you will find for the very first time is that deep within you a curiosity begins to emerge. In addition, this curiosity will not go away until you find some answers. The main objective is that everyone has to seek and search this information out for themselves. Personally, I call this the beginning of your journey towards self-discovery. However, never fear when those questions enter your mind, the right person (as a teacher) or the right book will be presented to you and will offer you the information you are seeking.

The wisdom of the Ancients states that, "**when the student is ready the teacher will appear**". Many have verified the authenticity of this statement.

When I was growing up, I remember very clearly two types of people that shaped my life. I refer to them today as the Martyrs and the Students of life. The Martyrs constantly complain about something or someone and everything is everybody else's fault, but never theirs. Therefore, I presumed at the time that they were unlucky and somehow life had short-changed them. In other words, they were somehow stuck in the mud for better or for worse. By the time I reached age 10 or 11, I realized that they had the victim mentality and the attitude to go with it. Another thing I noticed was that occasionally some people who had been living their lives as martyrs, for some reason, had finally had enough of playing the victim. **Within a short space of time**, their attitude and quality of life began to change for the better, and to my amazement, I found that it was then a pleasure to be around them. The type of people who are the Students/Seekers of knowledge always presented themselves to me as wise and compassionate people. They taught me very early on that if you want to become a successful and happy person you need to become a seeker of knowledge and gather as much information about life as possible. The most important thing they did was point out the difference between worldly possessions and gathering knowledge. When you are gaining knowledge, you also gain power. You can lose all your possessions at any time, but no one can take away from you what you have already learned. **That is forever**.

From the earliest years of my life that I can remember, I was naturally curious and a "seeker of knowledge". One day I realized that the more I learn, the less I know. The reason for this is because every subject within our world of realities and beyond is constantly evolving and this type of change can be referred to as the "never-ending story". After all this time, I gathered as much knowledge as I possibly could. If today anyone would ask me what I have learned so far, my answer will have to be the same as before: "Because the only thing I know for sure is that there is so much to learn and experience out there." **However**, I do know enough to share with you the wisdom I have already gathered, and I hope that you will be able to use it to change and improve your lifestyle for the better.

So let us begin our journey!

1st
CHAPTER

CONTENTS

- The Cosmic Map and its Hierarchy 8
- Universal Godhead and the 24 Elders 9
- The Realm of the 24 Elders and its Hierarchies 9
- The Planetary Logos and their Hierarchies 10
- The Seven Major Archangels 14
- The Cosmic Family of the Sun and the Twelve Signs of the Zodiac 16
- The Maintenance of the Human Body 19

The Cosmic Map and its Hierarchy

Cosmic Logoic Plane

24 elders that surrounds the throne of grace
(council of 12 for multi-universe)

Cosmic Monadic Plane

Cosmic Atmic Plane ***Mahatma***

Multi-Universal Monadic group

Cosmic Buddic Plane

Universal Monadic Council of the Melchizedek - Universal logos

Cosmic Mental Plane

Galactic Monadic - Universal Avatars

Cosmic Astral Plane

Planetary Logos

SANAT KUMARA

and it's Planetary Logos
and the Six Kumaras - Buddha's

Lords of Karma and the 7 Ray Masters

Astral Levels	Chakra Position	**Related Glands**	Governing Hierarchy	**Physical Realms**	Elements
8. Cognition	*Transauric*	**Pre-cortex**	*Elders*	**Omniverse**	*Akasha*
7. Mental	*Crown*	**Cortes**	*Masters*	**Universe**	*Fohat*
6. Spiritual	*Brow*	**Pineal**	*Governors*	**Galaxies**	*Ether*
5. Causal	*Throat*	**Thyroid**	*Directors*	**Nebula**	*Lipika*
4. Creative	*Heart*	**Thymus**	*Guardians*	**Solar System**	*Fire*
3. Intellect	*Solar-Plexus*	**Pancreas**	*Guides*	**Plantes**	*Air*
2. Emotion	*Abdomen*	**Adrenals**	*Free-Spirits*	**Nature**	*Water*
1. Energy	*Base*	**Gonad**	*Thought-Forms*	**Elements**	*Earth*

0. *Plane of Physical Existance and Visible Matter*

Universal Godhead and the 24 Elders

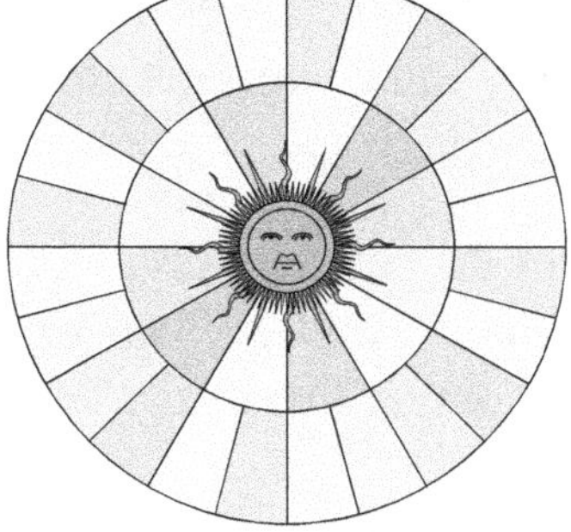

The Sun *representing the Supreme Mighty God Force*
The inner ring *representing the 12 Mighty Archangels*
The outer ring *representing the 24 Mighty Elders.*

There are 24 Elders, with the 12 Mighty Archangels and Associated Beings who have a close working relationship with the Supreme God Force of Intelligence. They are the only ones that can stand near the Godhead without being burned up and destroyed by the Mighty God Force. I would compare the Godhead and its immediate region to the heat of the Sun.

The Realm of the 24 Elders and its Hierarchies

The 24 Elders hold a very important position in the scheme of evolution. One of the tasks of the two gateways that deal with sending out and receiving the flow of information towards the Godhead, is to send this information out to the associated Cosmos, until it reaches the lower grade of dimensions of existence. (*Let's call these two gateways the post office of God*)

The Planetary Logos

Melchizedek
In charge of organizing the levels of the heavenly worlds
Co-equal with Metatron.

Metatron
Creator of the outer worlds and electrons.
Sanat Kumara and its Planetary Logos
With the six Kumaras-Buddhas

Sanat Kumara
Holds the blue print of evolution for Planet Earth.
He is in charge of the evolution of the mineral, vegetable, animal and human kingdoms. He is also in charge of the planetary hierarchy.

The Planetary Logos and their Hierarchies.

The majority of Ascended Masters were never re-incarnated into a three-dimensional physical existence, but some were. In the last two thousand years some chose to be born into a physical body, and played a very important role in the human evolution. Without their assistance and guidance we could not achieve self-realization. The most outstanding and well known by many today, are: Lord Buddha, Our Lady Mary, and Jesus Christ. But a few more need to be introduced to those who are just new on the Spiritual journey.

MELCHIZEDEK
This Master brings forth a great power for change both in individuals, and the planet itself.

LORD BUDDHA
The Master Lord Buddha bestows the richness of wisdom to all that have prepared to receive it. His radiating love resonates within you.

LORD MAITREYA

The Master Lord Maitreya serves the Divine Source in the role of Energizer of the Earth, and the Controller of the Solar System.

MASTER JESUS

Expresses the energies of the infinite Father of Unconditional Love. He awakens, within the heart chakra, the need to understand self-love and to be able to give and share unconditional love to others. Jesus Christ is also known as Sananda. He is the Master of the sixth ray–indigo. During his incarnation as Jesus, he was a high priest in the order of Melchizedek and was overshadowed during his life by Lord Maitreya. He works with Archangel Uriel to bring peace, brotherhood, and service to mankind.

KUTHUMI

The Master Kuthumi is an initiate of Wisdom and Love. He has a strong association with the Master Jesus and his teachings. He helps with those who work on self-awareness, and he bestows special energies in this area.

QUAN YIN

The Master Quan Yin is a Celestial Bodhisattva, the female aspect of Buddha. And she is also an Ascended Master. One of her jobs in the celestial spheres is to sit on the board of the Lords of Karma.

MASTER RAGOCZY

The Master Ragoczy offers assistance to those who are rigid in traditional concepts. His vibratory color is amethyst, which changes into the frequency of gold.

HILARION

The Master Hilarion has a vibratory color of bright yellow. The brilliance of such a frequency reaches into the darkest corners, where some of you may have transgressed, even to the depths of degradation. This Master helps with cleansing and healing the physical, mental, and emotional bodies, and brings light into one's darkness.

SERAPIS BEY
The Master Serapis Bey dispenses energies to those who work harmoniously with nature, and the healing of the Earth's environment. He is the Master of the Devic Kingdom.

PAUL THE VENETIAN
The Master Paul the Venetian operates from within the Golden Ray. He raises the consciousness of those of you who are interested in the study of the arts, music and practical sciences.

EL MORYA
The Master El Morya, assists those who wish to achieve self-awareness, and Spiritual enlightenment, and helps in the control of one's willpower and tolerance when life seems difficult. Also, for those whose interests lie in Astrology and Numerology, he offers his influence.

LORD MAHA CHOHAN
This Master brings forth communication to the Hierarchy and for those of you who have awakened spiritually, or are about to.

LADY NADA
This Master brings forth, and helps Humankind's overall needs, rather than wants. She helps those who have been drawn into misleading information generated by some traditional institutions. She also helps those who are inclined to be over-critical of themselves, to reach a more evenly balanced attitude within.

DJWAL KHUL
The Master Djwal Khul, whose vibratory color of emerald green, signifies the balance of positive thought and self-expression. He assists those of you who are interested in natural healing, and the usage of herbs. He also assists those involved in voluntary and welfare work.

LADY MARY

The Master Lady Mary, Mother of Jesus on Earth. She bestows the energies of intuitive wisdom upon those females who aspire to leadership within the community and in world affairs, and gives them courage to establish themselves in society. Also one will find her presence at every pregnancy and birthing. With Motherly love, she cradles the Spirit of the child-self within you.

LORD LANTO

The Master Lord Lanto offers assistance to those who feel drawn to a greater learning of wisdom, especially when the student desires to reach enlightenment. *I have only listed a few, but there are many more within the Hierarchical Government.*

I highly recommend the following books to read on this subject:

By Joshua David Stone, Ph. D.

- The Ascended Master
- Light the Way
- Beacons of Ascension

Archangels

Created as the Messengers of God.

The Seven Major Archangels are: *Michael, Gabriel, Raphael, Uriel, Raguel, Sariel and the Fallen Lucifer.*

Most religions recognize and accept that there are four major archangels, Michael, Gabriel, Raphael and Uriel. They are charged with aiding all humanity with protection, guidance, clearing of negative entities and lost soul attachments, healing of physical, emotional and mental pain. Archangels are able to be in many places at one time.

Archangel Michael

The first Angel created by God–Michael is the leader of all the Archangels and is in charge of protection, courage, strength, truth and integrity. Michael carries a flaming sword that he uses to cut through etheric cords and protects us from negative entities and lost soul attachments. Michael helps us to realize our life's purpose and he's invaluable to lightworkers helping with protection, space clearing and spirit release.

Archangel Raphael

Raphael is a powerful healer and assists with all forms of healing in humans and animals. Part of Raphael's healing work involves spirit release and space clearing. He often works with Michael to escort away negative energies, and lost souls from people and places. Raphael is known as the "Patron of Travelers" and assures safe travel. He also helps with inward spiritual journeys, assisting in searches for truth and guidance. He also assists with establishing healing practices. He helps you to heal from physical, emotional and mental pain; he also heals wounds from past lives.

Archangel Gabriel

She is a powerful and strong Archangel. Gabriel helps anyone whose life purpose involves the arts or communication. She acts as a coach, inspiring and motivating artists, journalist and communicators and helping them to overcome fear and procrastination. Gabriel also helps us to find our true calling. Call Gabriel if your body is full of toxins and needs purifying and if your thoughts are impure or negative and need clearing and cleansing.

Archangel Uriel

Uriel is considered one of the wisest Archangels because of his intellectual information, practical solutions and creative insight. Uriel's area of expertise is divine magic, problem solving, spiritual understanding, studies, alchemy, weather, earth changes and writing. He is the Archangel who helps with earthquakes, floods, fires, hurricanes, tornadoes, natural disasters and earth changes.

Archangel Raphael

He has been attributed as the chief of virtues, although that ranking has also been given to Michael, he can also be considered head of the guardian angels. He is also considered to be a patron of the sciences as well as medicine.

Archangel Sariel

Working alongside Raguel, his role is to decide the fate of angels that stray from God's path. Sariel was also the Angel of Death. It was claimed that Sariel was a healer like Raphael, a Seraphim and the Prince of Presence. He is also credited as being an angel of knowledge, and one of the leaders in Heaven's armies.

The Cosmic Family of the Sun, and the Twelve Signs of the Zodiac

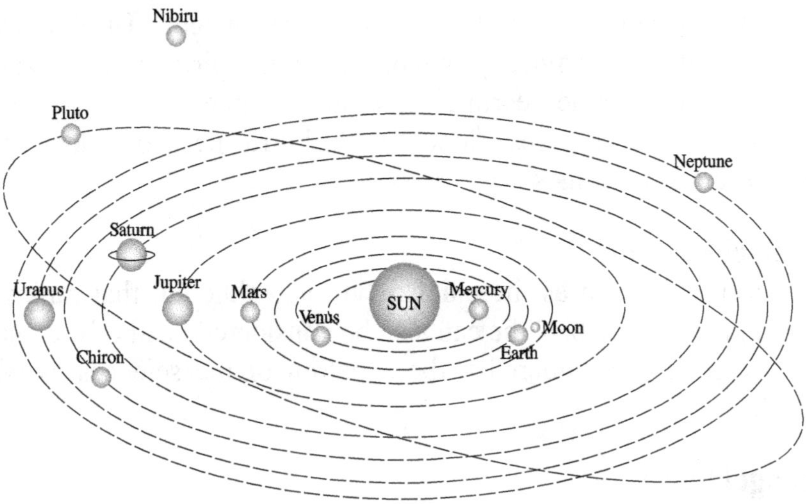

Well known Astrologer Alan Oken, the author of *Complete Astrology* described man's relationship to our Solar system and beyond as:

A child is the son of Man.
Man is the son of the Earth
Earth is a child of the Sun
The Sun is a child of the Galaxy
The Galaxy is the son of its super galactic parent

And all is One in the consciousness of the Father / Mother–Universe
The Divine Hierarchy began to create our Solar system according to the blue print that has been designed and laid down by the Supreme God Force and its Hierarchy.

The Master Teachers and Time Keepers

The third planet from the Sun was selected to serve as the school of learning for the three dimensional Soul's consciousness to evolve and to develop. All the planets within our Solar System play a very important function in the Soul's evolution. They are the **Master Teachers and Timekeepers** on a variety of subjects within daily events as they have governed the Soul's journeys throughout the ages. When an individual is born, there is a timetable that relates to the "blue print" that is given at birth. This "blue print" is referred to in astrology as the Natal Chart (birth chart) and contains within it all the lessons needed to be played out in a variety of scenarios during the Soul's current lifetime.

The Planets in the Solar System

Each planet is circling around the Sun, on its own pathway, each to their own timing, some moving more slowly than others. These are the planets in our solar system: **Sun, Vulcan, the Moon, Mercury, Venus, Earth, Mars, Jupiter, Saturn, Chiron, Uranus, Neptune, Pluto, and Nibiru**. (*Vulcan and Nibiru are yet to be discovered scientifically*.)

Earth is also surrounded by the 12 Zodiac constellations which include: **Aries, Taurus, Gemini, Cancer, Leo, Virgo, Libra, Scorpio, Sagittarius, Capricorn, Aquarius and Pisces**.

The 12 Classrooms within Your Natal Chart

Your blue print or in this case, Natal chart, is presented in the shape of a circle which is segmented into 12 segments that we refer to in astrology as houses, each house representing a facet of your personality. **The Planets** will take position in these houses as teaching Masters, and will visit each house, or classroom. Each Planetary master teacher has their own personality and subject to teach in every classroom when contained within the 12-house system. **The Planets** always work through the 12 zodiacs, they never work independently. (*I call this a husband and a wife team. The Planets as the husband and the wife the Zodiac*.)

The 12 Houses within the Natal Chart

The 12 classrooms represent the 12 major subjects you need to learn and excel in within this journey.

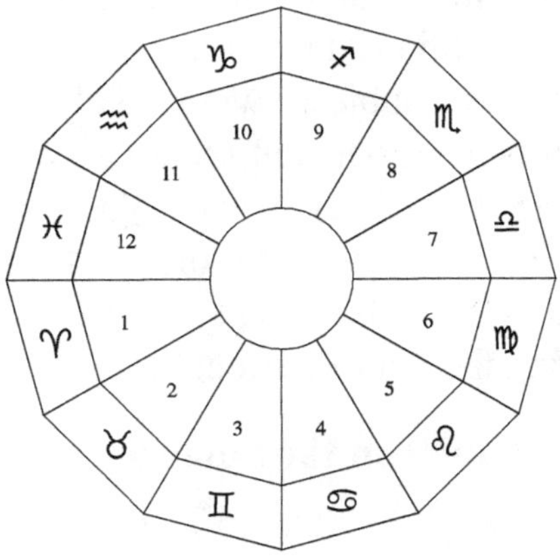

1st House–Self-image and expression and behavioral tendencies.
2nd House–Personal resources, material values.
3rd House–Inspirations, ideas, communication and ways of expression.
4th House–Home, domestic issues, parents and family.
5th House–Love, romance, kids, creativity.
6th House–Work, employees, personal service, health issues.
7th House–Open-adversaries, enemies, partners, spouse and "others".
8th House–Other people's resources, legacies and regenerative influences.
9th House–Philosophy and religion.
10th House–Public image, social contribution, profession.
11th House–Friends and associations, social values.
12th House–Hidden confinements, Karmic bank account.

When each planet passes through the houses it brings with it a certain lesson to be learned. Or, if you have already passed that lesson with flying colors, then this is the time when the student of Planet Earth will experience grace and abundance.

The Maintenance of the Human Body by the 12 Zodiac throughout the 24 hours of the day.

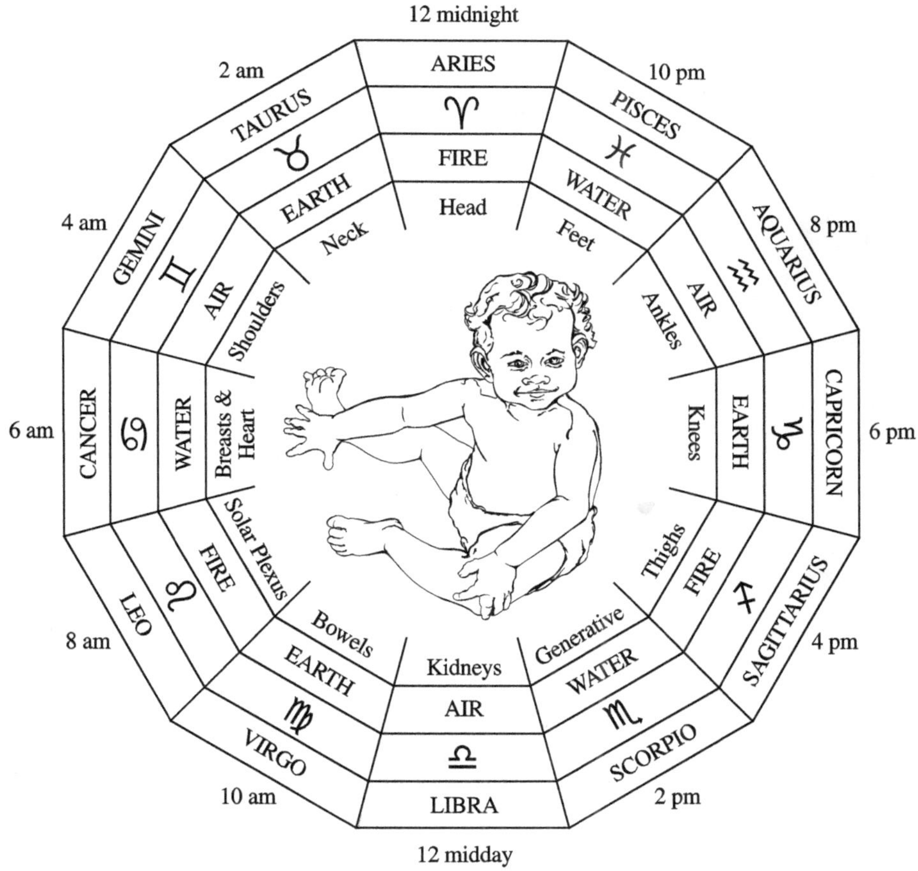

The **Zodiac** and the **Planets** are the **Architects** of the physical body, which is created according to the "Blue Print" of each individual.

Each sign of the Zodiac governs and maintains certain parts of the physical body, from midnight to midnight each day. The 12 Zodiac constellations will travel anti-clockwise, spending two hours in each sign around the Planet Earth, and directing its energy consciousness into our body. So, every two hours **each** and **every** part of your body is **maintained** and **revitalized** by a certain sign of the Zodiac.

2nd CHAPTER

CONTENTS

◆ The Family Tree of the Over Souls and its Egos 22

◆ The Birth of the Over Souls 22

◆ When the Higher Self Gives Birth to its First Child...................24

◆ The Soul Consciousness and its Present Personality 25

◆ Two Higher Selves and their Soul Extensions............................26

◆ The Twin Souls and Soul Partners 26

◆ The Three Categories of Relationships......................................27

◆ Self-Sabotaging Behaviour Pattern..28

◆ The Male & Female Genders 30

◆ Why Does the Soul Consciousness Choose to Become Homosexual? 33

◆ Why Does the Aids Virus Mainly Affect Homosexuals?............35

The Family Tree of the Over Souls and its Egos.

In order to describe the very complicated story of the manifestation of the family tree of the Soul concept and Higher Self and its Higher Ego and Lower Ego, I need to introduce this to you in a simple but comprehensive story. When the third dimensional solar system was finished, the only thing that was necessary for the God Consciousness to send forth was a large spark of Consciousness of its Self to experience and learn emotions in the physical three-dimensional Planet Earth School of learning.

The Birth of the Over Souls

By the time that spark had entered into our solar system, this spark of God Consciousness was almost as big as the Sun within our own Solar System. When this "spark" had reached the designated target point, the transformation was set in motion, by bursting itself into a number of larger sparks. Those large sparks of light individually began to transform and shape themselves into a large golden egg, and those golden eggs are called Over Souls.

The Over Soul Egg

The Higher Self Egg

Each Over Soul's Spark continued to burst into smaller sparks and each spark continued to transform into a smaller golden egg, and each golden egg is called a Higher Self.

Each Over Soul Egg is able to store (house) about two thousand Higher Self Eggs.

And each Higher Self Egg in time will be able to store (house) and give birth to between one to two-hundred individual Soul Consciousnesses.

A Higher Self will only be able to send down one spark of consciousness of itself the first time. This spark is called Soul Consciousness, and is also referred to as the Higher Ego. When the Higher Ego gains a physical body that will be referred to as the Lower Ego. The Soul Consciousness always maintains communication with the Higher Self, and never loses awareness that it is part of its Higher Self. The Soul Consciousness' (Higher Ego's) command seat is within in the 8th Chakra which is positioned right above the head. The Soul Consciousness is able to descend to the 4th chakra. The Soul Consciousness is also referred to as the silent witness.

When the Higher Self Gives Birth to its First Child

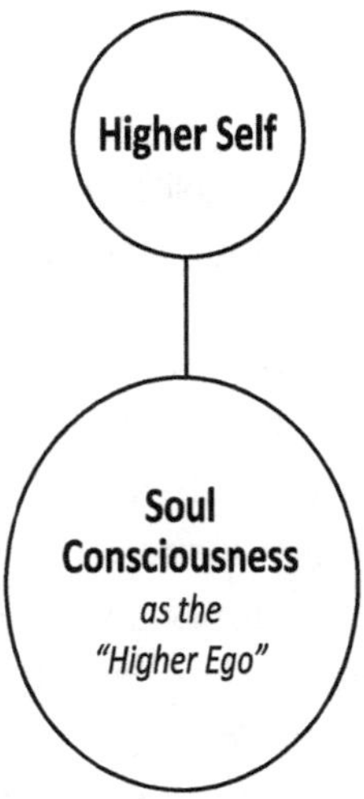

When the Higher Self is ready to send forth its first spark of consciousness into the physical reality, (*like a Mother giving birth to its first child*), this spark of consciousness is then referred to as the "Soul Consciousness, the Higher Ego".

Anything this child (the Higher Ego) is ever going to experience throughout its journey, the Higher Self will experience and learn from each experience as well. But it will not stop there, because whenever the Higher Self gains new experiences it will send this information up to the Over Soul and the Over Soul will send it up to the God head.

Then, at a later stage when the Higher Self is ready and it is sure that it can handle two Soul Extensions at the same time, (like for example send one Soul extension down into Europe and the other into China) it will bring home colorful experiences to the Higher Self. Remember a Higher Self can manifest between one to two-hundred Soul Consciousnesses.

Some Higher Selves are only happy to have a small number of Soul Extensions, to ensure the quality of learning. Other Higher Selves choose to have a big family just like an Earthly mother who has a large number of children and is still able to care for them and able to bring them up as very respectful members of society.

However this large number will not be born instantly, rather it will be spread out over a long period of time. All the children of one Higher Self are called Twin Souls.

The Soul Consciousness and its Present Personality

I would like to begin with a story and use it as an example. When we get up in the morning and start a day we usually get dressed first. Let's say that you have a large walk-in wardrobe. Every piece of clothing you have ever had from the time of your birth until now is hanging in your closet. Let's take this story to the next level and this time each outfit will represent one lifetime and each outfit will have a long story to tell.

Each time your Soul Consciousness is reborn it will have a new outfit, and will be referred to as the latest update of the Soul's Present Personality. This Present Personality will have to wear this new outfit throughout its journey. The Soul Consciousness will forget all about the other garments (past lives) that remain hanging in its heavenly wardrobe.

The Soul Consciousness and the Higher Self and its Spiritual Hierarchy devised this new dress and this new dress will contain the blueprint of this new journey, which contains some of the positive as well as negative attributes of previous past lives. The Present Personality will not be able to remember any of its past existence on Planet Earth, unless it's part of the plan. This way, the Present Personality will have a clean slate and will be able to continue its journey without remembering all the good or bad things he/she was doing in those past lives.

Two Higher Selves and their Soul Extensions Are Called "Soul Partners"

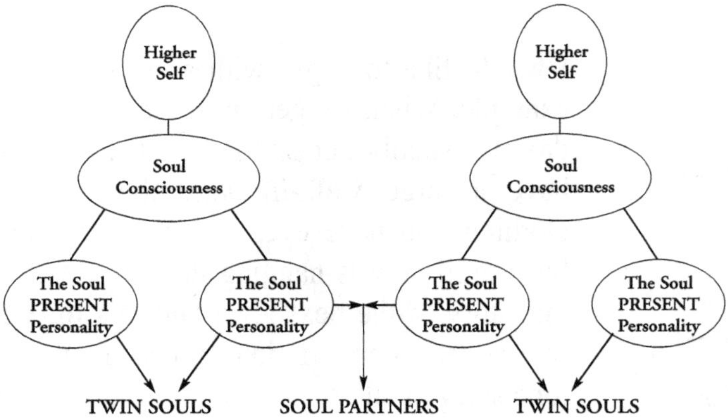

Relationships with your Twin Souls and Soul Partners

I have been a Tarot card and Palm reader for many years now, and the first thing most of my clients want to know is when they are going to meet their Twin Soul partners. Ninety-nine percent of the time they are already with their Twin Soul or their Soul Partners but, they do not realize that yet.

The Twin Souls and Soul Partners Relationships

Expectation from the public point of view the "Twin Souls" are supposed to possess the following characteristics:

• When you finally meet the love of your life, His/her will treat you like royalty and you will live happily ever after.

• From the first moment you laid eyes on one another and if you fell attraction towards one another that must be love. And the reason you believe this, because you must have shared a romantic relationship in past lives.

• You are convinced that with this partner you are not going to have any of the problems and hardships you have experienced with other partners so far, and this love will last forever and ever. (*it is a nice dream but may not happen at this stage*)

The Three Categories of Relationships

- **First category**—gaining experience and learning the hard way.
- **Second category**—gaining Knowledge and beginning to think that you can do better than this, and start making better choices.
- **Third category**—when some of your Knowledge turns into Wisdom.

The First Category—"learning *the hard way*"

For Example: when you and your partner share in this type of emotional partnership. You have not been able to speak about your feelings and your problems, and you keep expecting to be able to read each other's mind and know what is troubling each of you. If neither of you has the wisdom (and you seldom do at this point) and you don't realize that you need to communicate with one another, then the blame game will begin and you will start to accuse one another about anything and everything. Then very soon selfishness, jealousy and anger, emotional and physical abuse will be poisoning the relationship until one of the partners realizes that this is not good and they want out. But each partner will carry their unlearned and misunderstood negative behavior. The problem is that each partner will only be able to draw a partner into their life that has the same behavior patterns as they have at the present time.

For example if your relationship capabilities are resonating on number 3, you will only be drawn to that particular person who will also show an interest towards you and are also resonating on the number 3. You will never be able to draw the interest of those who resonate on the 4th or 5th level. You will know instantly that they are out of your league. If anyone shows interest in you and they resonate on either level 1 or 2 you would feel that they are not in your league, and you would walk away.

Where does this Self—sabotaging behavior pattern comes from?

Your parents will set the example for you from the time of your birth. When you chose your parents, you selected them because they have the same lessons to learn as you do. You relationship capabilities will resonate, lest say on the number 3 scales regards to relationship capabilities.

When you have grown up and ready to enter into your first relationships, you will not find it surprising if your partner treats you the wrong way. This sort of treatment will be normal and familiar to you and your partner.

You have both grown up in an abusive household. Neither of you like what you see or feel, but you don't know how to change this abusive behavior. And when somehow you are able to gain enough courage and walk away from one another, you will promise yourself that the next partner will be the best in the world.

The problem starts when you grow up and your hormones guide you in the name of love, you will be drawn to the same category of behaviors as your parents were. The name of the game is that you can break out of this mold any time. You only need to realize that you deserve better and can start learning new ways of how to go about obtaining what you want.

The second category of relationship

The second category of relationship can be described as "*I have been there done that many times*". When an individual reaches the next stage of intellectual self-awareness they will state; I have gained enough experience and enough **Knowledge** to know that I love and respect myself too much to allow myself to have a partner who only wants to abuse me emotionally, physically or mentally. Well guess what? You can just step forward and earn yourself a better partner. You will find that this person had a similar path as you currently have, and they are ready to change and are also eager to learn how to work on a relationship. No more playing the martyr and they are finally learning to stop blaming others for their own shortcomings.

So far you share relationships in the past with all those Twin Souls and Soul Partners and with some more than others. If you have reached the middle age Soul category, that means you have already been reincarnated least 100 times then from this point on, you are ready to progress to higher levels in relationships and you will find at least 10 perfect partners who are on the same resonating level as you. This type of "perfect relationship" is what you have been dreaming about from the very first relationship throughout all your life cycles, but you have to earn it first. Remember the wise statement "it takes two to tango" to be in a perfect partnership.

The third category.

The later stage of Knowledge and the beginning of the Wisdom stage.
Instant recognition of love for one another: This is the stage when your thoughts and desires are on the same page. No need to talk about it. It is the same, like twins! Only those who have progressed to this stage can bank on it that they will find the love of their life, and this can be achieved with one of your Twin Souls, or one of your Soul Partners.

Each Person Possess both the Female and Male Gender

When you live on planet earth two genders make up the human race.
*The **Female** and the **Male**.*
Both differ from one another in significant ways.

An author named John Gray wrote a book regarding the male and female differences. He made a point of the differences between the two genders by giving his book the title: "*Men Are from Mars, Women Are from Venus*".

In order for the Higher Self to experience each gender independently, the Higher Self made it possible by creating two genders in the first place. The Soul Consciousness is able to choose and change gender before each re-birth. What will take place is when you play one gender the other will be dormant during that particular life cycle. However, the dormant gender will still play its part when a situation occurs where it may be required to do so.

For example; As a **Male Gender**, when you show emotions, like crying, love, hate, compassion. Those basic characteristic traits are female.

As a **Female Gender,** when you show leadership and organizational abilities, these characteristic traits **belong to the male**.

Your Higher Self may choose to send down **its Soul Consciousness** to be born **as a male** for 3 times in a row. Then the next 3 rebirths it will be **as a female**.

After that the Higher Self will have an understanding of what is it likes to be a man, who needs to play the role of supporting his family financially, or to be able to love and share his life with a woman and love his children unconditionally. The reality and responsibility of his family's well-being will rest upon his shoulders. In the meantime he needs to learn and trust his dormant female aspect, and not to fear it, but work with it and not to look upon it like a devil angel who sits on one of his shoulders and guides him into trouble all the time. In a nutshell, when the Soul Consciousness plays the role of the male he needs to perfect all those lessons and allow himself to live in harmony with his female side. Until they learn to live in harmony with one another they will have a long and painful road ahead.

Teachers will be lined up for the male to teach him how to understand his female side, and those teachers are going to be; Mother, sisters, their wife and later their daughters and any other females that will enter into their lives. Each and every one of those on the list will teach you the many facets of your feminine side.

When you born as a Female: each and every one of those on the list will teach you the many facets of your male aspects and you will have different lessons to learn.

The most important lesson as a female will be giving birth to a child and being able to care and look after it for a long time. This act will demand pain at birth and self-sacrifice, and lots of patience.

With the birth of the first child the female will experience for the very first time the feeling of unconditional love. The role of mother or father is hard but yet very rewarding. It takes a few lifetimes before they will be able to look forward to becoming parents.

Unconditional love is a very unique bond. The only people who share this type of bond are both parents, and their children. When the conception of the child has been fulfilled both parents and the child will be connected to each other within the heart chakras by the cord of unconditional love. That is the only reason children sometimes can get away with blue murder, and the parents will only be able to see them as little angels who cannot do anything wrong in their eyes.

As a female you also need to learn to stand on your own two feet. Do not allow others to make a slave out of you in the name of love. Each time you need to stand up for yourself you must behave with respect toward your opponents. If you allow your emotions to take you to the point of no return, the male aspect is there for you to teach you how to keep a lid on your emotions and to think before you react when this happens. Eventually, when you manage to create harmony between your female and male aspects, this will the time when you will feel that you do not need anyone to complete you.

That does not mean you need to live alone and not share your life with someone in a loving relationship. The difference will be that you are both together because you love one another and not because you need to depend on each other.

Teachers will be lined up for the female to teach them how to understand their male side, and those teachers are going to be; your Father, brothers, boyfriends, husband, sons, etc. Each and every one of those on the list will teach you the many facets of your male side.

Why does the Soul Consciousness Choose to become Homosexual?

I would like to begin sharing this important and very necessary information with the public. Homosexuals have constantly been persecuted and disrespected by the whole world in general. Unfortunately, the human consciousness has not yet evolved enough to know better, and to be able to treat them equally like any other members of our society. But we are learning every minute of the day. And I am hoping that by shedding some light in regards to this type of gender, people will be able to change their point of view and in time behave with respect towards the homosexual society. I would also like to make it clear that I don't have any hidden agenda in writing this information about homosexuality other than I am someone who has access to some very vital information in regards to this subject and I believe the time has come to let the public know about this third gender that is part of our evolutionary cycle.

First of all I am a "straight person". I have been married and have given birth to two children. I never felt any romantic feelings towards the same sex. The information I am sharing with you comes from being a conscious channel from the Akashic Records, and when I read the blueprint from my clients' palms. Also I have been teaching Metaphysical Spiritual Self-awareness classes for many years. But in the last 4 years I have transferred this knowledge and wisdom I have learned so far and chose to share it with a wider audience by writing a book.

Previously I explained the reason why the Soul Consciousness needs to change its gender. For example: if the Soul Consciousness takes on one gender too many times, let's say 10 or more times in a row, and really enjoys playing the role of the female or male part, then the next time when the Higher Self says it's time to change gender in the next rebirth the Soul Consciousness will agree because the other gender has been left behind in the process for too long. However, he/she really enjoyed playing the former gender and it's a difficult transition into the new gender this time around.

So the baby is born as a male physically, but as he is growing up somehow he does not feel he is a male, but a female. He feels that "she" is trapped in the male body. What has really happened is that the Soul Consciousness could not let go of being a female gender from previous lifetimes. The memory is still very female oriented. And this Soul Consciousness was not able to put its female gender into a totally dormant state. Both genders are then active in this life cycle.

Most people have seen or spent time around homosexual people. And they have all experienced their emotional ups and downs. When a homosexual person gets emotional about anything they will burst out like a tornado and their emotional outburst will be equal to three females' outburst put together. When we look into the art world you will find homosexual artists on the top of the list. They are simply the best in this field, or any field they choose to be in. They will win hands down all the time. The very reason they are able to be the best is because they have the two worlds from both sides of their gender, because neither side of their gender is in the dormant state.

The best way for me is to give you an example, just visualize this: if all the **straight people** in the world (*meaning they present only one active gender*) had to walk on crutches because one of their legs is stiff, *(the other gender being dormant)* and because of this ability they need the aid of the crutches or a walking stick to walk.
On the other hand, the homosexual people *(both gender is active)* walk freely on both feet.

Now I will expand on this subject a little further. Remember the statement that "**As Above, So Below**" and that secondly within the higher realms the Soul Consciousness consists of the male and female called IT. In other words both genders are active within the spirit realm. That is its nature. Everything within our solar system is based and consists of the trinity.

Example;

• The Soul Consciousness within the Spirit Realms **as Male & Female**—referred to as **IT**

• The Soul Consciousness on Earth as— Female gender; **dormant Male**

• The Soul Consciousness on Earth as—Male gender; **dormant Female**

• The Soul Consciousness on Earth as—Male & Female; both genders are active and we refer to them as **Homosexuals.**

Homosexual gender represents the Soul Consciousness in the Earthly state as the Physical IT!

I believe the third aspect of the Soul's evolution belongs to the third gender that we referred to as homosexuals. Which brings me to the conclusion that when a Soul Consciousness chooses to be born 10 or more times to that particular gender it's not done by coincidence, but there is a very important reason why this occurs. And that reason is to be able to create a situation that both genders can be active in at the same time just like "As Above, So Below" This way the learning for the Soul Consciousness will be harder to endure.

Why does the Aids Virus Mainly Affect Homosexuals?

In our society due to sheer ignorance, homosexuals are persecuted by the general public. The public labels them as rejects and misfits of our society. When a young person realizes for the very first time that he/she is homosexual, they feel they have to hide it from their parents, friends and the world. They begin to feel dirty, ashamed, and guilty. All these negative feelings about themselves will be stored and processed within the person's base chakra. (*Please refer to the auras & chakras*)

The **base chakra** represents a very important function in the human body. This is a center (office), which is dealing with and processing all the experiences and feelings to do with procreation and sexuality, and the will to live. When your base chakra keeps registering negative information such as self-doubt and hatred and shame etc, then it will have no choice but to send an S.O.S message to the heart chakra.

The **heart chakra** represents love for self and others.
The request from the **base chakra** to the **heart chakra** will be as follows: "in order to function properly I urgently need you to send me self-love and respect otherwise I am going to be out of balance. And when I am out of balance I cannot maintain physical well-being, and I will lose my will to live."

The **heart chakra** will reply back, "I am sorry I have the same problems as you do; my heart is full of self-hatred, fear and misery".

The third chakra positioned above the **heart chakra** is called the **immune system chakra**. This chakra is responsible for your general health. Protecting you from all diseases and illnesses throughout your life. When this chakra is invited by the other two chakras for an emergency meeting, to see if anything can be done the **immune chakra** will announce "if self-hatred settles in both of you, I cannot keep the physical body safe from any disease for very much longer. And after this meeting the AIDS virus will have free passage and attack the body".

Many times I have advised my homosexual clients that it's up to them to gain the upper hand on the illness of AIDS by simply accepting who and what they are. And to realize that they have a very important place in our cosmic creation. The name of the game is self-love, when they are able to love themselves they will never fall prey to the AIDS virus.

This is the very reason that I have shared this vital information and shed some light on this missing link, regards to the third gender as homosexuality of the Higher Self evolution.

3rd CHAPTER

CONTENTS

- The Akashic Realms 38
- The Karmic Lords and the Governing Hierarchy 38
- Planning the Itinerary for the Soul-Extension Before Birth 40
- The Farewell Party 41
- Before Conception 43
- When the Life Cycle Comes to an End.................................... 44
- How Long Can a Lost Soul be Part of a Living Person's Life?..47

The Akashic Realms

The Akashic Realms Reside within the Last Band of the Earth's Auric Field. Planet Earth is a living entity, and also emanates its own energy field. From the first layer of the Earth's auric field, each layer (dimension) is lighter and higher in vibration, as it goes up through the eight astral planes. This last band of auric field is called the Akasha and its colour is gold. This is the lightest, highest energy. This is from where the Ascended Masters govern our physical and Spiritual development. Also, you will find here the Akashic library, which contains each and everyone's life history from the beginning of time.

The Karmic Lords and the Governing Hierarchy

The Karmic Lords of Light represent an office of Ministry within the Akashic Realms, which is responsible for supervising and overseeing every Soul consciousness in progress, according to the plan of each and everyone's blueprint. Their expertise and function is crucial. Without this Ministry, the Planet Earth School of Learning cannot function. The members of the Ministry are many. They include the Ascended Masters, the Brotherhood of White Light, and a range of other Planetary and Galactic beings that wish to provide a service such as this. There are various levels of expertise, and accordingly, many offices exist to handle each level and dimension of situations, which relate to the governing of Planet Earth.

For example:
One of these offices is a fully staffed Ministry, which only deals with the Soul Consciousness that is ready to be reborn again. The delegated Karmic Lords will sit in conference with the Higher Self and the appointed Soul Consciousness. This is to plan out the next itinerary, also referred to as Blue Print, in accordance with the planetary movements, and their learning needs.

The second delegates of Karmic Lords may only deal with those Soul Extensions that are **about to pass over** from their physical existence. The appointed Guides and Archangels will facilitate this Soul extension to step out of their physical body of reality, so that they can escort them to their destination. This place is called the "*Hall of Arrivals*" and the Soul Extension will be welcomed home by all the previously passed over relatives and beings that have been overseeing and taking part, to a certain degree, in their three-dimensional Earth journey. The Karmic Lords also have a Ministry office, which will monitor and keep a record of your progress, regarding the ways you use your three levels of consciousness, (your Conscious, Subconscious, and Super Conscious mind) and your Free Will. In other words, each time you make a decision your reactions in any situation in general, will be recorded and graded by your appointed supervising Guide structure. They present a service to you by strictly recording every thought-form, desire, action and reaction in every moment.

The Moon and its cycle play a very important function in our daily life and have power over our emotional body. When the **New Moon** is about to appear, your Governing Master teachers will present your progress to the Karmic Lords. Your progress will be examined until that moment in time, and accordingly your next cycle will be set in motion until the next New Moon. **Between each New Moon we also have the Full Moon**. In this Moon phase your progress of activity will also be on review, but this time the difference will be that rewards for positive or negative consequences will be given for your past actions. You may recognize this as your prayers have been answered, or all the doors of opportunities closing before you when you are about to enter.

You Are Also Given a Passport That is Called "Free Will".

Now you have been given "free will" to choose and decide how to act, behave, or deal with anything, or anyone, when a situation presents itself.
But, the consequence of your decisions and behavior for "better or for worse" is also yours to bear! This action is called "cause and effect". In Sanskrit it is called "Karma". Remember that how you treat others, you will be treated as such! Eventually, the Lords of Karma will see to that!

Planning the Itinerary for the Soul-extension Before Birth

When you, (*as a Soul extension*) are ready to begin and continue your education at the Planet Earth School, according to your learning needs, the Karmic Council of Light and your Higher Self will devise a blueprint, (*your itinerary*) from your time of birth to the passing-over stage.

Your Itinerary will include:

- **Selecting** a country in which you need to be born
- **Selecting** your parents, and your immediate family members
- **Selecting** your future relationships as spouses
- **Selecting** your friends and teachers
- **Selecting** your children, to have or not to have
- **Selecting** a career within the work force
- **Selecting** your financial situation: whether you will be rich, poor, or only just have enough.

Each major subject will have its own guide structure that will be responsible for that particular subject, and to see when you are ready to be upgraded each time. Then the next guide's shift will take over. You will recognize this in your present daily life, as you suddenly want to do certain things, which you previously had no desire to do. When this sudden change of desire occurs, this usually signals that you have progressed and the next shift of Guide structure is taking over. This shift change will take you higher to the next level of your learning.

For example: when you attend school, each year your teacher is different from the previous year. And when a new teacher takes over a subject, it is taught to you at a higher level. This is also the case with the Guide structure.

A Master being will be selected to be your gatekeeper, to oversee everything that is going to take place in your life according to your blue print timetable. You will have an agreement, (*exchange of contract*) with anyone with whom you may have to spend more than five minutes in your life's journey, allowing you to teach and learn from one another in the Earthly School of Life.

Gatekeepers seldom change and each Soul Consciousness will have the same gatekeeper for many re-incarnations to come. The gatekeeper is in charge and keeps its eyes on anyone who wants to enter into your world without prior arrangement. And when someone enters without a calling card, the gatekeeper will deny them entry.

The Farewell Party

When the Soul Consciousness is ready to be re-born, and the blue print has been completed, the Soul extension is invited along with the other Soul extensions (which are about to start their journey to Planet Earth School) to a farewell party. At this party they are served a very potent drink. This beverage will be served as a "memory block" of the Soul's true identity as a Divine being, and it will also block out all past life memories. After the party is over they will all fall into a deep sleep. The Soul extensions are then placed **in the re-birth pool** to await the appointed Astrological alignment and the chosen parent to be ready, so the pregnancy can take place. When you are born, you will not have any memory of your past lives, until you return back to the astral planes again. That is, unless it is part of your itinerary to progress Spiritually on Planet Earth and due to Metaphysical advancements you will gain the grace to remember your true identity and your past life history.

The Rebirth Pool

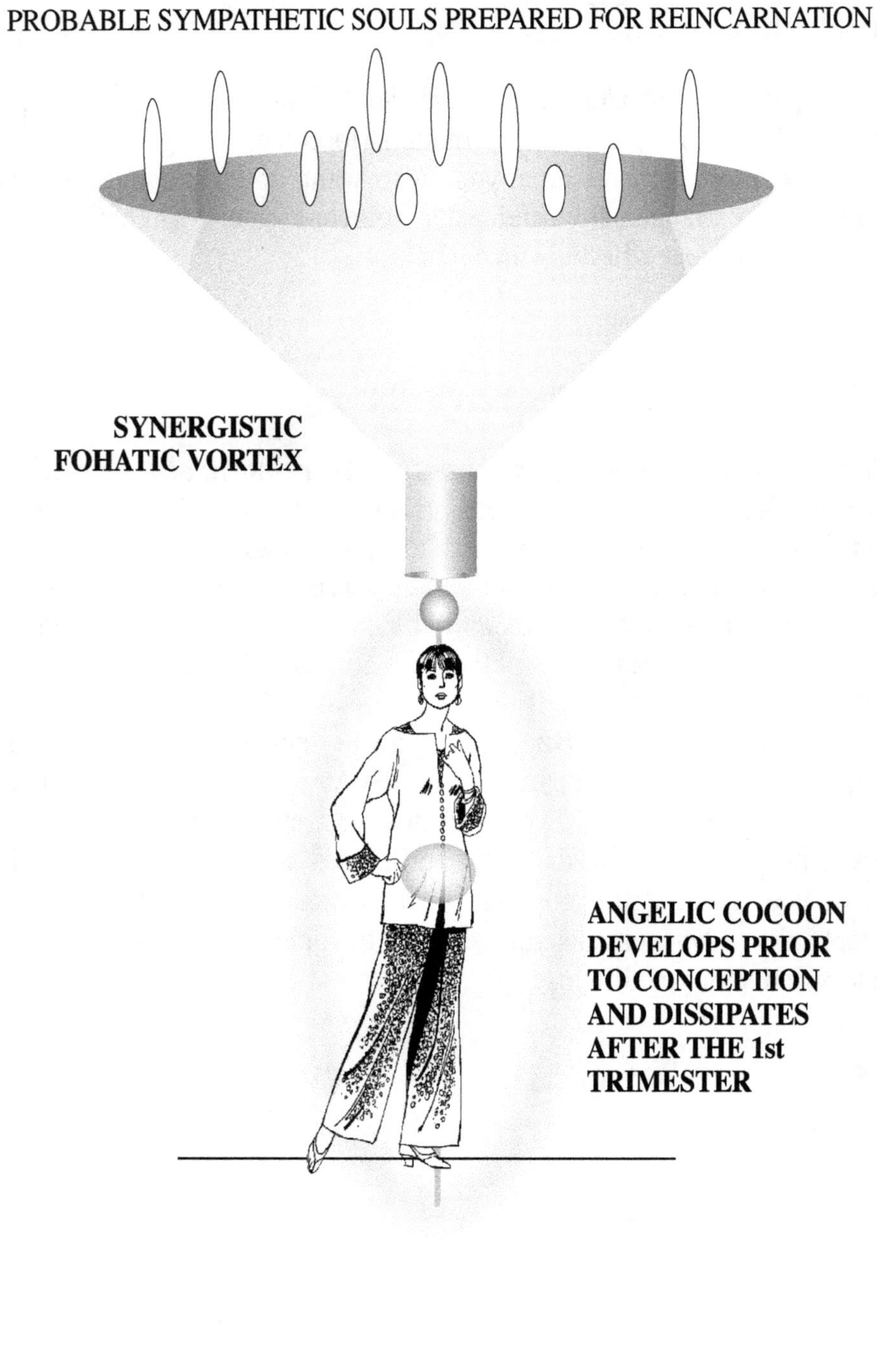
PROBABLE SYMPATHETIC SOULS PREPARED FOR REINCARNATION
SYNERGISTIC FOHATIC VORTEX
ANGELIC COCOON DEVELOPS PRIOR TO CONCEPTION AND DISSIPATES AFTER THE 1st TRIMESTER

Before Conception

Six Weeks before Conception the Soul Consciousness will have attached itself, with a cord of light, to the chosen mother-to-be.
Within the mother's womb the first preparation takes place. The womb is filled with pink light by the Angelic realms and its divas, to accommodate and nurture the incoming Soul extension and to assist manifesting into the physical reality.

The Time Requirements for the Soul Extension's Birth and Departure.

For a baby to develop and to be born, it takes about nine months, plus the six weeks before conception.
Before you are about to pass-over, it will also take about one year to prepare the mind, body and Spirit for departure.

For example: if a clairvoyant sees a person, who has not much time left in the physical body, they witness this person's aura as though the colors are fading out; the colors do not look as vibrant as those who are not ready to pass over yet.

What the clairvoyant will see above the person's head is energy fizzing upwards, like the rising of champagne bubbles in a glass. In other words, the Soul Consciousness is gradually withdrawing from the physical body. In the last five to six days, this person has hardly any colour left in their Aura. There is only a black nothingness surrounding them. Some people have a long life to live and others just a short period of time. Very few, a small percentage, will pass-over before the appointed time. And when they do, it is because the Higher Self has decided to terminate the Soul consciousness.

Two reasons the why the Soul Consciousness can be recalled:
The first reason–is because the Soul Consciousness was a good student and learned everything in a shorter space of time than was needed. And it

is possible that the Higher Self has a new project for this particular Soul Consciousness.

The second reason–is because the Soul Consciousness has gone off from the original blueprint, and it was wasting its time. Just like any student who is wagging school.

When the Life Cycle Comes to an End.

When we finish each life cycle, we step out of our physical body. The associated Guide structure and the Angelic force, which are responsible for this type of service to humanity, in general, supervise this. Then you will be escorted into the "tunnel of white light". This will transport you to the astral plane, and its allocated sub-layer of your destination. This sub-layer of your destination is selected according to the progress that you have achieved, up until this point in time. The "tunnel of light" will take you to the arrival chambers of the Karmic Council, to evaluate your progress that has been achieved on the Earth School, at this stage. You will stay in the astral world, and spend a lot of time in the hall of learning until you are ready to continue your earthly education again.

The Reality of the Lost Souls

Physical death occurs when the Soul Consciousness draws its last breath and is ready to step out of the physical body. For some people who have no understanding, or have never had any interest in the concept of the Soul Journey, this can be a very dramatic situation, of which they have no understanding or the memory of experiencing in this life. (Oh if only they would watch the movie "***Ghost***", which starred Whoopi Goldberg, Demi Moore and Patrick Swayze, they would recognize the situation instantly!)

When the Soul steps out of, or is ejected from the physical body, the person still sees and feels themselves as solid, as their dead body, which lies in front of them. They try to jump back into their former body, but to no avail. It feels cold and alien. They cannot be one with their body as before. So they have no choice but to step out once again. They may suddenly see and recognize relatives, doctors or nurses, trying to shake their former physical body back to life, but it does not work.

In the meantime, this poor, lost, confused Soul is standing there trying to speak to them, but no one is listening, or paying any attention to them. **To the others**, this Soul has just become invisible and they are busy trying to revive this physical body that is in front of them!

Suddenly a bright light comes towards the Soul, with the intention of beaming it up and this may frighten them even more, especially when previously passed-over relatives come toward them. The passed-over relatives are here to welcome the recently passed over Soul and they are ready to show the way. **But** the lost Soul suddenly remembers that the relatives are already dead (ghosts) and they themselves are not (according to their own understanding); they are ready to run away from these beings as fast as their feet can carry them.

The white light will try many times in the next seven to ten days to pick the Soul up, and take them to their destination. But the Soul usually doesn't know or understand why this white beam is chasing them, so they run as fast as they can away from it.

A new and strange world will be surrounding this person, which can be very scary at first. The world around them has changed dramatically. Day and night blend in to one another and semi-darkness surrounds them at all times. All the colors have disappeared from everything. They soon find out that they can walk through solid buildings, people and anything else that was in the former physical world, which they just recently left behind. Their friends and relatives and every living person ignore them completely, as if they have become invisible to them. And in reality, they actually have become invisible.

The second stage of this reality is that they then realize that those people, who have been so rudely ignoring them all the time, are surrounded by an oval-shaped bright light, which looks very warm and cozy. This light is what we call the Auric Egg of each individual. When the Lost Soul walks near to those people who have strong bright light surrounding them, they cannot stay too close because the bright light can burn them just like when they would look into the sun. So they make a mental note in the future to stay away from them. They also discover another type of people, whose auric light is dirtier in colour. Some even have holes in their Auric Egg due to drinking excess alcohol, or from using drugs. The Lost Soul realizes that they have no difficulty in standing near this type of person. And for the first time the Lost Soul realizes that he/she is not alone. Many lost Souls attach themselves through the auric holes of the living person.

In the meantime, the Lost Soul discovers that whatever thought they think suddenly manifests instantly and that by wanting to attach themselves to a certain individual that thought will instantly manifest as a dark rope, or a tentacle, and they are able to attach themselves to other people's Auric Eggs.

This is going to be a lot of fun, because they have found a new way to survive within this strange world. Now they can share and tap into other peoples' light. The reason they do this is to harvest energy so that they can stay alive. (They do not realize that when they stepped out of their physical body, they no longer need to consume food to keep them alive.)

The Lost Soul still has hunger pains, and if they were an alcoholic or a drug addict, they will still have the same cravings. The reason for that is because when they stepped out of their physical body, their Soul consciousness still continued to wear their Astral/Emotional bodies. That is the reason they still feel hunger, cravings, etc. So, later on they will seek out those humans who are on drugs or drink alcohol and urge them to drink more, and they will tap into their energy to share and feed their own habits. **But**, this will not usually satisfy them for very long, even if this newly found energy of survival might give them the impression that they are alive. Plus they are getting the best entertainment into the bargain. It gives them a power thrill knowing that they can interfere in someone's life, and make them do what they want.

How long can a lost Soul be part of a living person's life?

The situation cannot be predicted because each case is different. This type of possession happens to many people. Most do not realize that some of the emotional problems they have do not even belong to them. When someone begins to learn Metaphysical understanding and starts
to learn meditation they usually purify their emotional body, and regain control little by little.

Then usually the Lost Soul cord attachments will be detached by the Karmic Angels, who will be able to take them to their destined place.

When the lost Soul is rescued, it sheds the Astral body, and arrives at the chamber of the Karmic Lords of Light, in the appointed sub-layer of the astral plane, they will begin to remember what has happened to them, and their full memory will eventually return. For the Soul it feels like they have just woken up from a nightmarish dream, and suddenly it dawns on them that it was only a dream, and nothing more. They then realize that nothing can harm them, because it was only a dream. The Karmic Lords of Light are ready to revaluate the progress and the achievements of the Soul extension as the graduate of the Planet Earth School.

The next step will then be that they will have to attend the Hall of Learning for some time before they are ready for the next journey.

In the late 1980's a new gateway opened up.

This gateway is available for those to send through lost Souls to their destined places and on to the appointed astral planes and its sub layers. This means that anyone who practices regular Meditation, and "boogie busting" techniques is able to send any lost Soul through the gate.

You may ask, why would anyone provide a service like this? Firstly, by helping others to go through the gateway, you will enable them to realize their own Divine Self and understand that they are merely a student who forgot the way home. They will no longer need to attach themselves to anyone for survival, and can progress forward on their evolutionary cycle.

Secondly, the more lost Souls you send through the gate, the fewer will be left to interfere or to be an influence in anyone's life and their emotional behavior. So a big service is done all around!

The "BOOGIE BUSTING" technique to send the lost Souls through the gate is included in the Meditation.

4th
CHAPTER

CONTENTS

- When the Soul Consciousness is Ready to Descend into a Physical Existance (re-birth) **50**
- The Human Aura and the Seven Major Chakras **51**
- The Spiritual and the Physical Chakras **52**
- The Seven Astral Planes – The Seven Major Chakras, and the Seven Year Cycle of Change... **55**

When the Soul Consciousness is ready to Descend into a Physical Existence, (re-birth) it will receive:

- **The 8 Layers of Auric field**
- **Chakras**, as the communication and record keeping and administration centers.
- **The Mind** and its three levels of Consciousness
- **And** "Free Will"

When the Soul Consciousness is ready to descend into a physical existence, an energy transferring **lift will take** the Soul Consciousness down to visit each astral plane.

Each Astral plane will gift the travelling Soul Consciousness with a very special "robe" to wear. Each astral plane's elemental components, "robe" is made out of that element and will contain part of the blue print, which refers to that particular astral plane's learning. The robe is referred to as the layer of the auric field.

The AKASHIC REBIRTH Plane		Elemental "Robs"
8th PLANE	The 8 CHAKRA	AKASHIC ELEMENT
7th PLANE	CROWN CHAKRA	FOHAT ELEMENT
6th PLANE	THIRD EYE CHAKRA	ETHER ELEMENT
5th PLANE	THROAT CHAKRA	LIPIKA ELEMENT
4th PLANE	HEART CHAKRA	FIRE ELEMENT
3rd PLANE	SOLAR PLEXUS CHAKRA	AIR ELEMENT
2nd PLANE	2nd CHAKRA	WATER ELEMENT
1st PLANE	BASE CHAKRA	EARTH ELEMENT

With each robe, (auric layer) the Soul Consciousness will receive one pair of chakra and one is placed in front and the other at the back of the body.

The Human Aura and the Seven Major Chakras

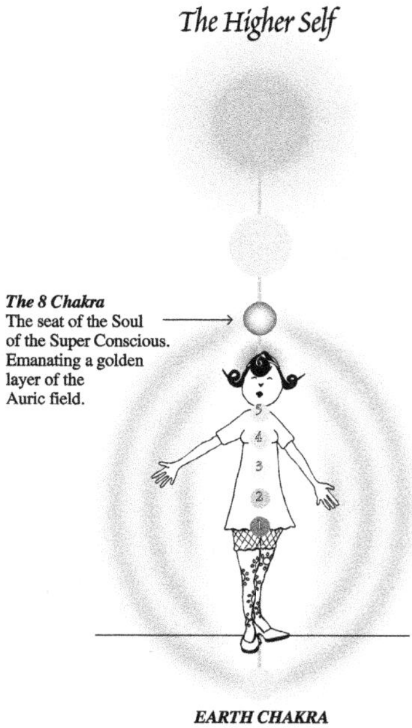

Around the human body there is an oval shaped energy field. This energy field in Esoteric Science is called the "**Auric Egg**" which stands out from the body about 1 to 1 ½ meters on average on all sides, above the head, and below the feet penetrating into the ground, and finishing below your earth chakra.

Your aura is a field of blended energies that emanates from your seven major chakras, which are located from the top of your head to the base of your spine. Each chakra has an associated color that expands within your aura.

Each Chakra's function:

- **A chakra functions** as an administration office and communication centre between the Governing Hierarchy of this particular astral plane
- **Each chakra contains** within the seven-color ray of consciousness, and seven sub-layers and seven dimensions.
- **It holds part** of the blueprint and its timetable, which is applicable to each chakra, and executes that a certain situation must take place at the appointed time.
- **It functions** as the centre for dealing, executing and recording all the new events that will take place throughout the person's life.

The Spiritual and the Physical Chakras and Their Associated Glands

All the chakras that are situated on the front of the body are called the Spiritual Chakras, (*the front office*)

All the chakras on the back of the body are called the Physical Chakras (*Back office and storeroom*).

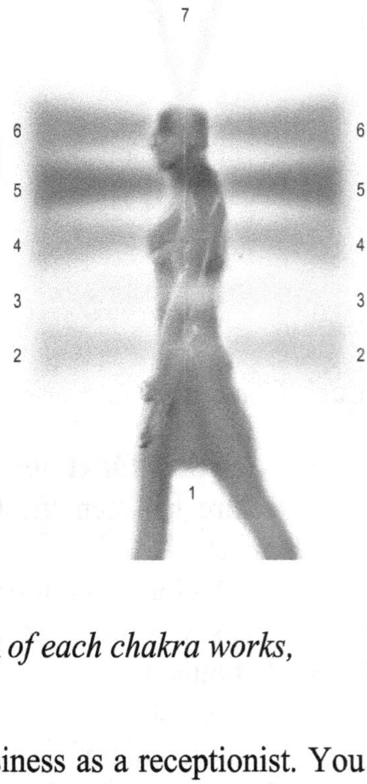

These chakras handle all the new incoming scenarios, and hold them there for no more than forty-eight hours. If the issue has not been dealt with positively after forty-eight hours have passed, the front chakras have no choice but to hand it over to the physical chakras to deal with.

The back chakras (*the back office*) will keep the situation for the next twenty eight days, after that if no positive solution has been found for this particular problem, the chakras have no choice but to pass it on to the associated organs.

In order to understand how the **front** and **back** *of each chakra works, I would like to use this story as an example.*

Let's say that you are working for a small business as a receptionist. You have been caught in traffic and you arrive one hour late to work. In the meantime, a few people had been answering the phone until you arrived. One of your colleagues, whose usual job is to deal with orders and selling, is having a very bad morning, and as soon as you step through the door she starts to accuse you of not passing on an important message to her. So because of that she has found herself in a difficult situation. You do not have any idea about this message. You try to tell her that but she never gives you a chance to say anything in your own defense.

Your reaction will be as follows: first you will be **shocked** then **surprised**, then you will get **angry**, and finally you will **feel helpless** regarding this false accusation. Within half an hour you will be called into the office, and your boss gives you an instant dismissal. He is not interested in hearing what you have to say in your own defense. You have to pack your bag, and leave the premises instantly.

You will go home in shock and dismay, and go over every single moment of what has just taken place that day. This scenario keeps you up all night and day, and probably will for the next forty-eight hours. All the feelings and sensations you have experienced will register within two chakras at the same moment as the situation takes place.

And those chakras are the Solar plexus and the Emotional chakra **Solar plexus** is also referred to as the **3rd Chakra** and is located below the sternum, which is known as the Solar–plexus.

Governs: the Intellect, your understanding of the world around you.
Associated gland: pancreas When more and more negative emotions and anxieties pass into the pancreas, this will cause the organ to be blocked and will prevent the organ from fully functioning as it did before and therefore a variety of illnesses will develop as time goes by.

Associated physical illnesses to this chakra affect the digestive system, liver and gall bladder, and at a later stage can cause cancer within the pancreas.

The Emotional Chakra is also referred to as the **2nd Chakra** and is situated below the belly button.

Governs: the emotions, relationships, to give and to receive.

Associated gland: adrenals.

Source of stress: Your adrenal glands respond to every kind of stress whatever the source may be. For example: physical stress–such as overwork, lack of sleep, or emotional and mental stress and anxieties.

Associated physical illnesses: hormonal imbalances, tendency to gain weight and diabetes. One incidence will not cause any of those illnesses mentioned above, not even one life cycle will produce those results. In order to manifest such an illness these events have to occur over the course of a few lifetimes. And when the person is not able to learn from each event and they keep accumulating those negative and painful memories within the organs, eventually they will manifest into major illnesses.

The Seven Astral Planes
The Seven Major Chakras
And the Seven-Year Cycle of Change.

The Soul Consciousness Dons the First Garment (robe) Which was created out of the Elements of Akasha And also receives the Associated Chakras.

The Eighth Chakra has two colors, gold and white, and is situated above the top of the head, about 30 cm high on average. **It is connected** to all the seven major chakras and also to the higher chakras up to the Higher Self.

This chakra is also referred to as the Seat of the Soul, or the Trance Personal Point, or the domain of the Super Conscious Mind.

The golden light emanates from the eighth chakra, encasing the human body and its seventh layer of the auric band. It is contained within an oval shape, and is referred to as the "Auric Egg". According to the belief systems, desires and thoughts of each individual, the Super Conscious Mind will arrange whatever you believe and need, *(within in the contents of your blueprint)* and will draw in the right people at the right time to work with one another to gain that particular experience you both need and believe in at that point in time.

Because of this process, the saying states that:

The Super Conscious Mind
Will Rearrange Itself to Suit Your Purpose of Realities.

For example: If you believe that you do not deserve to be happy, and that something is wrong with you and that you are not good enough to have someone who may possibly love and respect you for who you are, then this type of thinking and these beliefs about oneself can only draw the type of people into your life who will play the part and prove that you were right in the first place.

The Super Conscious Mind will broadcast this information out loud and clear as if using a loud speaker, and will magnetically draw to you **only** the eligible relationships which have the full potential and capability to prove to you that you were right. They will prove that you are not good enough to be loved or to be respected and so on and so forth and treat you accordingly.

Have you ever heard this wise statement before? That "like attracts like". In other words whatever you believe about yourself, positive or negative **your Super Consciousness has no choice** but to bring those people into your life to prove to you that you are right. When you have experienced enough bad relationships and as soon as you make up your mind and realize that you deserve a better partner, your Super Conscious Mind has no choice but to change your relationship frequency and move you up to the next level. Once there, next time you will be provided with better partners.

As the wise saying states:

"If you want to change your world, **You** *need to change your thinking."*

The Soul Consciousness Dons the Second Garment (robe) Created out of the Elements of Fohat. And also Receives the Associated Chakras.

- **The 7th Chakra–the one thousand lotus petals**
- **Location:** at the top of the head
- **Colour**: purple,
- **It is the seventh layer** of the auric band called the mental body
- **Governs**: integration of the Mental and Spiritual Aspect
- **Associated gland**: pineal
- **Associated organ**: brain
- **Ruling planet**: Vulcan and Pluto

Leadership between: 42-49 years
This is the first centre that is touched by the cosmic energy coming from the higher self through the higher chakras.

When this chakra is opening (*beginning to function on a higher resonance*) gradually you begin to realize that you are not your emotions or the physical body, but you are the spirit who lives in the body.

As one of the wise beings stated that you are not one person, but three:

The one you think you are: **the Physical**
The one others think you are: **the Mental**
And the one you really are: **God**

When this chakra is blocked life becomes stagnant and depression ensues.

The Soul Consciousness Dons the Third Garment (robe) Created out of the Elements of Ether And Receives the Associated Chakras.

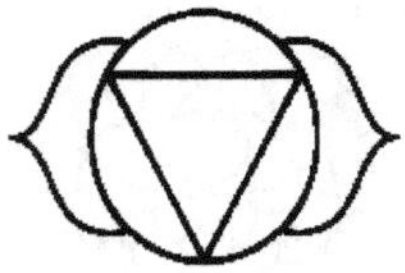

- **6th Chakra contains of 96 petals**
- **Location:** between the eyebrows, and also referred to as the "Third Eye"
- **Colour**: indigo, the sixth layer of the auric band, called the Spiritual centre
- **Governs**: the Concepts of Spirituality, and God, and communication to the higher realms.
- **Associated gland**: pituitary
- **Associated organ**: eyes, ears, nose
- **Ruling Planet**: Venus

Leadership between: 35-42 years.
This chakra is the spiritual centre. It controls the day and night visual within your eyes. It receives and interprets messages from the spiritual higher realms, and understands mental concepts.

When this chakra is open: the person will be able to manifest their creative ideas into physical reality. They also begin to develop clear astral sight.

When disruptions occur: mental and psychological distress, sleep disorders, confusion, hallucination, delusion, eye problems and hormonal diseases will ensue.

The Soul Consciousness Dons the Fourth Garment (robe) Created out of the Elements of Lipika And Receives the Associated Chakras.

- **5th Chakra has 16 petals**
- **Location**: at the hollow of the throat
- **Colour**: sky blue,
- **The fifth** layer of the auric band, referred to as the Causal body.
- **Governs**: vocal expression, sense of respect for self and others
- **Associated gland**: thyroid
- **Organ**: vocal cords
- **Ruling Planet**: Earth and Saturn
- **Leadership**: from the age of **28–35**

This Chakra is referred to as the communication centre. We communicate outwardly with others, and inwardly with ourselves. The sound of our voice is a weapon.

The wise ones state that "*With your words you can heal, and with your words you can kill.*"

When people are unable to speak, or to express their feelings for a long time, this will cause relationship problems in the long run. This seven-year cycle is also known as and referred to in astrology as "Saturn Returning" or in Metaphysics the "Karmic Zone Time". This will force the person to change and transform their out-dated values and belief systems regarding life in general.

Positive: Taking responsibility, successful within work and relationships

Associated illnesses: thyroid, slow metabolism, stuttering.

Outward symptoms: Seeing the world as a negative place, feeling disrespectful to others and self, hostile, violent. Will attract negative like-minded people.

The Soul Consciousness Dons the Fifth Garment (robe) Created out of the Elements of Fire and Receives the Associated Chakras.

- **4th Chakra has 12 petals**
- **Location**: at the centre of your chest
- **Colour**: green
- **The fourth layer** of the auric band called the Astral body
- **Governs**: love for self and others
- **Associated gland**: thymus
- **Associated organ**: heart
- **Ruling Planet**: Sun and Jupiter
- **Leadership**: from the age of **21-28**

This is the centre where we learn about the varied types of love for others and ourselves.

These seven years belong to the heart chakra, and the subject of the lessons to be learned will be the philosophy and reality of love. We all experience love in many forms and situations from the time we are born. **But** the difference is that before the age of 21, we experience love unconsciously (by instinct). Then as we approach the age of 21, we have gained enough experience in this field, and for the very first time we begin to understand what love is all about, and we are able to tell the difference between unconditional love and conditional love. Within the next seven years the Soul Consciousness will be making important decisions based upon self-love and respect. If one does not pay attention to this, then the result can be that you settle for second best and the wrong types of relationships, work, etc.

The heart chakra is also the transformer of the incoming cosmic energy, which enters through the crown chakra and when it reaches this centre, the heart chakra will transform this high vibration into a lower vibration of energy, which will enable it to send this energy to the physical chakras below. The heart chakra also transforms the upcoming lower physical vibration energy that comes from the earth through physical chakras. The heart chakra will transform the lower vibration into a spiritual energy and then send it up to the crown chakra and to the Higher Self.

When disruption occurs: this type of person will have the tendency to withdraw from society, they will not be able to trust or accept love or compassion. They will also come across as a cold, selfish and uncaring personality.

When this chakra is opened: the person is respectful to self and others. And most of the time they will not settle for second best. You will find those people will be there to help others and to be a guide and become teachers on the spiritual path.

Associated illnesses: asthma and lung problems

The Soul Consciousness Dons the Sixth Garment (robe) Created out of the Elements of Air And Receives the Associated Chakras.

- **3rd Chakra has 10 petals**
- **Location** below the sternum, and is called the Solar plexus
- **Colour**: lemon yellow
- **The third layer** of the auric band, called the Intellect.
- **Governs**: comprehension and understanding of situations and the world around you
- **Associated gland**: pancreas
- **Associated organ**: stomach, liver and gallbladder
- **Ruling Planet**: Mars and Neptune
- **Leadership**: from the age of **14-21**

Puberty:–almost overnight they think they have somehow become smarter than their parents, or any other adults for that matter. At the age of 16 the teenager will fight for their personal independence and demonstrate expressions of creativity. The reason this is taking place is because the time has come to cut the dependency on the energy cords between parents and their teenager. This means that from this time onwards, the teenager will become responsible for their own actions and bear the consequences. From the time of birth until the child's sixteenth birthday, any right or wrong decision a child has made that the parents have allowed to be carried out, will result in the parents receiving a double folded karma.

The first fold, because as a parent they should have known what consequences a certain situation can bring, and they still allowed it to take place.

The second fold of karma involves whatever the child suffered as a result of the bad decision so the parent will now also suffer in the same way. In other words, the parents are responsible karmically for the child until the age of 16.

When disruption occurs: timidity and fear, powerful drive to express anger and rage. Immoral drive and excessively driven by their ambitions.

Outward symptoms: hypoglycemia, diabetes and a variety of gynecological problems.

The Soul Consciousness Dons the Seventh Garment (*robe*) Created out of the Elements of Water And Receives the Associated Chakra.

- **2nd Chakra has 6 petals**
- **Situated**: just below the belly button
- **Colour**: orange
- **The second layer** of the auric band, called the Emotional body
- **Governs**: the emotions, relationships, give and take
- **Associated gland**: adrenals
- **Associated organ**: spine
- **Ruling Planet**: Moon and Mercury
- **Leadership**: from the age of **7-14**

For the very first time the child will be able to interpret the emotional world around them. They are beginning to understand the variety of relationships, self-validation and they start learning how to behave and understand the difference between right and wrong.

Positive symptoms: mentally and intellectually well-balanced, high achiever, friendly, happy and outgoing.

When disruption occurs: the lower digestive system is affected and this causes imbalance and disease.

Outward symptoms: general lack of vitality, rapid loss of youthfulness, loss of interest in life, and they stop attracting others into their life.

The Soul Consciousness Dons the Number Eight (robe) Created out of the Elements of Earth, And Receives the Associated Chakras.

- **1st Chakra has 4 petals**
- **Location**: at the base of the spine
- **Colour**: red
- **The first layer** of the auric band, called the physical energy
- **Governs**: the will to live, and houses the Kundalini and female and male forces. (Ida & Pingala)
- **Associated gland**: gonads
- **Associated organ**: reproductive system
- **Ruling planet**: Uranus
- **Leadership: 0-7 years**

The base chakra will take leadership amongst the other chakras from the time of birth until the age of seven. The baby will grow faster during these seven years than at any other time of their life cycle. They will have unlimited energy, and go through many childhood illnesses to develop their immune system to protect them later on in life.

For example, the base chakra will be responsible for maintaining the physical body in illness and in health. For instance, when we get sick or get the flu, the base chakra will alert the kundalini (page.) to begin raising the body heat to a high temperature and burn up the invading virus. The kundalini functions by raising the body temperature to the highest level the body can stand, and then it will repair the damage the virus has already caused in any part of the body. We refer to this type of heat commonly as a fever.

The base chakra also alerts the **immune system chakra** to get into action. The working relationship between the two chakras is imminent. And in the long run it provides the human body with healing and maintenance throughout the person's life cycle.

Conscious awareness of this chakra: when you experience a shiver from cold, heat, pleasure or the hair standing up on your body, or when you experience pain or overwhelming happiness.

Blocks within the chakra: deep insecurities and immune system malfunction.

Outward Symptoms: feeling the world is against you and feeling the need to fight back. A compulsive personality and greediness. In regards to sexuality, in extreme cases impotence or frigidity.

The First Astral Plane and its Seven Colors and Seven Sub–layers of Consciousness

Each Sub-layer Contains within the other six colors and its seven levels of consciousness.

The Seven *Sub-Layers*	*The Seven* *Colours*	*The Seven Levels of* *Consciousness*
1st Sub-Layer	**Red - and** ***the other 6 colours***	Wellbeing of the physical body **and** ***the other 6 levels of consciousness***
2nd Sub-Layer	**Orange - and** ***the other 6 colours***	Understanding emotional feelings **and** ***the other 6 levels of consciousness***
3rd Sub-Layer	**Yellow - and** ***the other 6 colours***	Intellect and comprehension **and** ***the other 6 levels of consciousness***
4th Sub-Layer	**Green - and** ***the other 6 colours***	Self love, accepting love and loving others **and** ***the other 6 levels of consciousness***
5th Sub-Layer	**Sky Blue - and** ***the other 6 colours***	Communicating and verbal expressions **and** ***the other 6 levels of consciousness***
6th Sub-Layer	**Indigo - and** ***the other 6 colours***	Spirit World **and** ***the other 6 levels of consciousness***
7th Sub-Layer	**Purple - and** ***the other 6 colours***	Mental concepts **and** ***the other 6 levels of consciousness***

Every Chakra in our physical body represents the same principle. First it has its own color, then it is contained within the other six colors, and within each color are the seven sub-layers of Consciousness.

The first chakra–located on the base of the spine–dominating color Red, and its Seven Sub-layers of Consciousness.

In order for any issue to pass the grade in any of the Sub-layers of consciousness, and then to be able to move up to the next chakra level of the sub-layer, it needs to pass within each chakra first.

Think of each levels of consciousness being like seven judges, and they have to decide and give their stamp of approval in order to pass or to fail the issue they have been presented. Their judgments will be based upon the person's past and present progress.

Here is a story to show you how each level of consciousness will deal with a scenario after it has taken place.

Steven is 29 years of age and right now he is in his fifth seven-year cycle. Recently he decided to become a professional ski instructor. He just barely passed his final exams, but he loves skiing. When he was skiing down the snowy mountain he slammed into a tree trunk. He
regained consciousness in the hospital, and received the news that his right shoulder had been broken, and his right leg had also been broken in many places. He was told that there was a very strong possibility that he may have to give up skiing altogether.

How will the Seven Levels of Consciousness Judge this Scenario?
First chakra, 1st sub-layer, color red, (physical)

This sub-layer governs the function and maintenance of the physical body. It can be maintained by eating the right food in moderation, regular exercise, and listening to the body when it says to stop pushing it beyond its limits.

The Red Judge states: the owner of this body has been looking after himself, and eating the right food, and he practices regular physical exercise. This judge is happy to approve the decision that this body must be healed completely.

First chakra: 2nd sub-layer, color orange, (emotional)
This sub-layer governs emotional issues, such as falling and hurting oneself, or when someone says hurtful things. This person needs to gain some clarity of understanding, otherwise that painful event can be held within the associated gland or organ inside the body as a block. This situation will then prevent any healing and maintenance in certain parts of the physical body, and will remain so until the issue has been dealt with and resolved permanently.

The Orange Judge: will state that the owner of this body was emotionally upset and his mind was on other issues, and because of that he was not able to pay attention to what he was doing at the time. When a warning was sent out to him advising him to stop, he simply ignored it. This is a recurring problem and this person has difficulty managing his emotions, and keeps ignoring his inner guidance and warnings. In this case, the judge refuses to give a passing grade on this issue.

First chakra, 3rd sub-layer, color yellow, (intellect)
This sub-layer represents the intellect of the physical body function, like a solicitor in a Court of Law. It has the ability to argue and defend and make deals with the other six judges.

The Yellow Judge: will say in defense that this person has been progressing well so far and the emotional issue was very serious. He will state that they should go easy on him this time around. If they cannot agree to pass him, his body will be sick and it can take a long time before he will be healed. But this judge cannot give a passing mark just yet. He has to wait for the others to decide first.

First chakra, 4th sub-layer, color green, (unconditional love for Self and others). This sub-layer governs the ability for self-love and protection, and self-respect. When you care for and love yourself enough, you will make sure that you eat the right food, or drive carefully, and be mindful of the people you have sexual relationships with and also avoid any harmful relationships.

The Green Judge states: he loves sport and activity, and loves the sport of chasing the opposite sex. He does not think or care about any consequences. The only time he is able to experience deep love is when he is engaged with someone sexually. I cannot give a passing mark; he needs to learn self-love and respect for this body.

First chakra, 5th sub-layer, color sky blue, (verbal expression)
This sub-layer governs verbal and physical communication. The physical body's language takes place when communicating its pain or pleasure. Also, when sending you a feeling of warning regarding danger or happiness that may be about to take place.

The Blue Judge states: I have been warning this person to pay attention to me. Sometimes they push me beyond my capabilities. And when I need him to take a pain killer he refuses to do so. This is good in the long run, because it enhances my physical endurance. But what I do not approve of is when he takes unnecessary risks. This type of behavior is not new according to my records going back through the last four lifetimes. This issue also bears Karmic consequences. So I believe this time around he needs to have a wakeup call, and I cannot pass him.

First chakra, 6th sub-layer, color indigo, (spiritual understanding)
This sub-layer governs the spiritual self-knowledge and understanding of the spirit and of physical realities.

The Indigo Judge states: This person looks after his physical body and because of that the three major forces are able to maintain his body, which was at his peak before this situation took place. But I cannot pass him at this stage, because so far he has only identified himself as a body, and he has no idea or inclination about his true identity as a spirit. So I cannot give him a passing mark. It is time for him to look deeper into the meaning of life. And if physical pain will make him do this, then so be it.

First chakra, 7th sub-layer, color purple, (mental)
This sub-layer governs the integration of all the seven sub-layers.

This is an ongoing process at all times, from the time of birth until the last second of passing over.

The Purple Judge states: Since the majority of you cannot pass this person, I have no choice but to turn the cosmic force down a notch. This will stop the body from healing fast, and it will also have a hard time healing. It will take two times as long to heal compared to others.

As you can see each subject will need to pass through all the seven levels of consciousness. The final decision to manifest as an illness will be decided within the base chakra first for any physical illness that you may have, or that you are ever going to have. So to know how this is done, you must remember the three major energy forces, the male/female and Kundalini are housed within the first chakra. The wellbeing of the mind/body/spirit rests upon the flow of these three forces. When any of these forces are blocked, the human body is unable to heal quickly and some organs will develop illnesses. I hope you will have a better understanding by now of why it takes so many lifetimes to complete and graduate from the Planet Earth School of Learning. The sooner you take responsibility for your actions, and realize that everyone is a teacher and a student at the same time, the faster you will progress within your journey.

How can we recognize progress in our daily lives? For example, we are all born into this world with certain abilities that are outstanding, and no one needs to teach us how to go about it, we just know. For the last century we have been hearing stories about young people who at an early age have the inner knowing that they have an important destiny to fulfill. Some will have a hard time paying much attention in school. However, they know within themselves, that when the time comes they have places to go. All the capability and expertise that they possess within this lifetime to be a successful business person, or a famous dancer, architect, author, etc. has been earned during several past lifetimes, and they have accumulated extensive experience, which has turned into knowledge. This presents itself now, in this lifetime, as well earned wisdom. That is the reason it looks and also feels as though it is effortless for them to perform that particular task and to be very successful at it.

5th CHAPTER

CONTENTS

- The Male and Female Energy Forces 74
- The Pathway of the Female and Male Force 75
- The Three Major Life Forces...76
- The Cosmic and the Earth Energy Breathing 77
- The Kundalini Life Force and the Symbol of the Caduceus.......79
- The "Three Knots" as the Three Gateways................................80
- Warnings and Guidelines Regarding the Kundalini Rising........81
- The Pathway of the New Master Teacher or "Guru"..................82
- The Maintenance of the Four Bodies...85

The Male and Female Energy Forces

The Base Chakra houses within.
The **Male** the **Female Gender** and the **Kundalini** life forces.

These three forces travel through channels or tubes, and in Sanskrit they are referred to as "**nadis**". The female energy is called "**Ida**" and the male energy is known as "**Pingala**". The **Shushumna**" channel, which refers to the spine, contains the **Kundalini** energy which flows when it is awakened. Regardless of which gender you belong to, your body contains **both** the male and the female energies.

The "Pingala" male channel corresponds to the left side of the brain, the colour is electric blue, and it is governed by the Sun.

The "Ida" female channel corresponds to the right side of the brain, the colour is pink, and the Moon governs it.

The "Shushumna" channel is for the Kundalini energy, which lies coiled within the base chakra, sleeping and waiting to be aroused. It then travels up the spinal cord and through the seven chakras, towards the source from which it has originated in the first place: the Higher Self.
When the Kundalini rises up and enters into the eighth chakra above the head, it begins to radiate like the Sun. The ancients described this experience as the thousand-petal lotus, the state of "Samadhi" which means bliss.

When you are born as a female, your Higher Self will place the male force into a semi-dormant state under the female force of command. The male force will only be active when events call for it. Like for instance, when you need to use rational thinking, logic, or give orders, organize things and take charge, etc.

When you are born as a male, your Higher Self will place the female force into a semi-dormant state under the male force of command. And the female force will be active only when you find yourself in a position to nurture or to care for someone, or to show compassion and love to someone, or express yourself through artistic expression.

The Pathway of the Female and Male Force

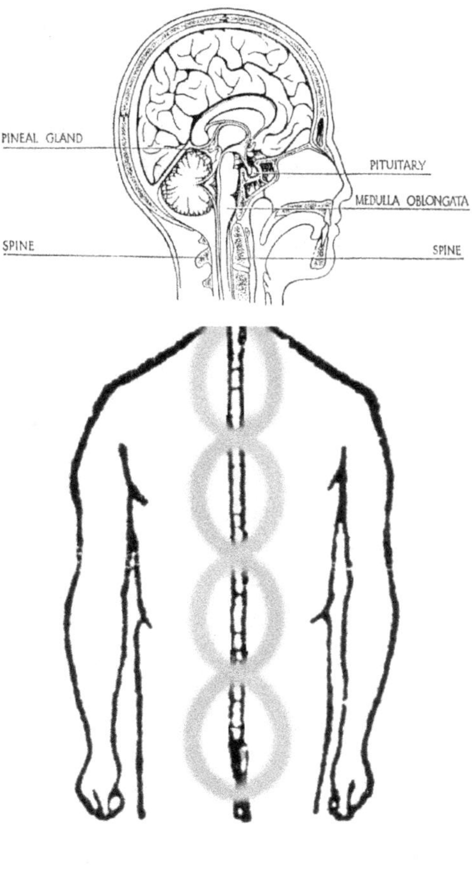

Both Gender forces intertwine between the chakras, each chakra will be encased in a circle of its own, one half of the circle is pink, and the other half is blue. These intertwining male and female forces apply to male or female alike.

Within the Female body the female force start out from the right side of the base of the spine, and move up along the spinal column and intertwines upwards between each chakra like a snake (energy tube), until it finally reaches the back of the skull, and enters the left side of the spine into the medulla oblongata. The **male force** within the Female body starts from the left side of the spine and begins its journey up along the spinal column and intertwines itself between each chakra like a snake (energy tube) and when it finally reaches the base of the skull, it enters the right side of the spine, into the medulla oblongata.

The feminine aspect of the force is responsible for feelings of nurturing, caring, compassion and love.

The male aspect of the force is responsible for taking charge, leadership and protection.

The Three Major Life Forces

The three major life forces are: the Cosmic Spiritual energy, the Air, and the Earth energy.

The Air we breathe in and out through our nose is also referred to as "the life giving force", or the "breath of God." The breath flows through the two channels, the "Ida" as the female, and the "Pingala" as the male channel. The two "nadis" or channels are constantly stimulated through alternately breathing through the left and right nostrils, which would alternately stimulate the left and right sides of the brain. If you add some special breathing techniques to this rhythmic breathing, it will influence the flow of the "nadis" or channels. The breathing techniques will purify and develop the two channels and eventually lead to the awakening of the kundalini.

The Cosmic Spiritual Energy flow enters through the Crown chakra and flows down through the upper spiritual chakras until it reaches the heart chakra. The heart chakra will transform the higher spiritual energy vibration into a lower energy vibration, and send it down to the lower physical chakras, and finally into its earth chakras.

The Spiritual chakras within the body: the crown, third eye, throat and the heart chakra. **The Physical Chakras**: solar plexus, 2nd chakra and the base chakra.

The Earth Energy from the centre of the Earth travels up and enters into to our physical body through our Earth chakra first, then enters through the soles of our feet chakras, and continues to travel upwards into the base chakra. It continues to move through the second and third chakra until it reaches the **heart chakra**. In this centre, the earth energy will be converted into a higher vibration and will continue to flow upwards to the immune, throat, third eye and the crown chakra, and then pass through the next chakras upwards. Each time the earth energy passes through a chakra, the energy will be transformed into an even higher vibration than the last one until it reaches the Higher Self.

The Cosmic and the Earth Energy Breathing.

Your body also breathes through the crown chakra and your earth chakras. This type of breathing happens naturally, and you are not aware of it consciously, only subconsciously. When you start your meditation, and begin to breathe the cosmic and earth energy consciously, your meditation will benefit from this type of breathing more than you can imagine. This breathing exercise used to be taught in the Ancient Mystery Schools, and in our times, in Yoga.

The Cosmic Breathing Exercise
You will need to repeat this breathing exercise three times. Always count when you take a breath from the crown chakra.

Please make yourself comfortable by either sitting on a chair, or on the floor, or just standing. Close your eyes,–put your conscious awareness above your head, where your crown chakra is situated,–imagine that your crown chakra has two opening slits that behave like a pair of nostrils, these nostrils will be able to breathe the cosmic light in, and breathe out the Earth energy just like your nose.

Now turn your conscious awareness towards your feet,–and visualize that the left and right soles of your feet are also manifesting a pair of nostrils, so they can breathe in and out. I would like you to bring your conscious awareness back to above your head.–You will notice for the first time that a radiant white beam of light is positioned about 5 cm above your crown chakra.

In reality you still breathe through your nose, only in your imagination you breathe through your "chakra noses."

I would like you to take a deep breath of that white light **through your crown chakra**–and hold your breath and visualize as the white breath of light as it travels down through each chakra until it reaches the heart chakra.–And as you are ready to breathe out–you push the white light downwards through the lower chakras,–when you reach the base chakra the white light will separate into two parts– and continue to flow through the left leg and the right leg.–Out through the soles of your feet into your earth chakra–into the earth.

This time you will **breathe through the soles of your feet**,–the radiant light will travel upwards along your legs–and enter into the base chakra and travel upwards through your 2nd and the 3rd chakra, and into the heart chakra– as you are ready to breathe out–with your breath out you push the light upwards through your throat, third eye and out through the crown chakra. **You then** begin breathing through the top chakra again, until you have completed the three sets of breath intakes. After this breathing exercise you can begin the meditation of your choosing.

The Kundalini Life Force and the Symbol of the Caduceus

The Caduceus is a winged staff, with two serpents.
The Caduceus symbol is still used and known today as the symbol of healers and medicine.

The snakes intersect at the chakras, as do the male and female energy channels. At the "third eye chakra" between the eyebrows, there are two petals, one on either side, just like the two wings on the caduceus.

The Angelic wings symbolize a superior degree of consciousness and mind. As a whole, the caduceus symbolizes regeneration and enlightenment, in other words, the attunement of the mind of man with the Cosmic Mind.

The Kundalini is linked to the image of the serpent, which is coiled up below the base of the spine.

The Kundalini has been referred to by many names throughout the ages.

In Chinese it is called the **Chi**, meaning: "present in all matter"
In Indian it is called **Prana**, meaning: "the energy life force"
In Greek it is called **Pneuma**, meaning "universal energy"

When the kundalini awakens due to spiritual practices like practicing meditation, yoga and the correct lifestyle to go with it, then the Kundalini force surges up through the chakras, and makes a person fully aware of their own spiritual divinity.

Regardless of what religious or spiritual tradition one may follow, sooner or later the awakening of the Kundalini energy is necessary to gain spiritual self-realization. The person will experience an instant awakening and a complete transformation, reaching the absolute height of spiritual realization, and having all their past lives' karma removed.

The "Three Knots" as the Three Gateways.

The gateways are referred to as "**knots**". The Kundalini must pass through the three gateways before it is allowed to continue to flow through the crown chakra and up to the eighth chakra, to the Higher Self. The "**three knots**" are placed in the **base, heart** and in the **third eye** chakras.

The first "knot" within the base chakra is when a person is able to transform their physical and emotional negative attributes, such as anger, hate, lust and envy etc and a safe passage for the Kundalini is given to rise upward.

The second "knot" within the heart chakra, will transform and allow the Kundalini to pass, but only if the person is able to master the concept of unconditional love for self and for others.

If not then the Kundalini will gently settle back into the base chakra, until the next time. But if the "knot" has been successfully transformed, then the passage for the kundalini will be open, and it can safely move upwards towards the third knot.

Within the Third Eye chakra if the person successfully transforms their mental desires and is able to transform the Lower Ego's wants and needs and its ruling tendency, **the third "knot"** will be able to grant passage to the Kundalini to flow through the crown chakra and up to the eighth chakra and beyond. When one breaks the third knot one does not need to come to this earth, except by choice to help others.

Warnings and Guidelines Regarding the Kundalini Rising

When a person is ready and is showing an interest regarding the Spiritual path, they will seek out anyone who has knowledge and offers guidance. Many teachers in this field will be very happy to guide the seeker. The only thing I can compare this type of education to is to a candy store. So many varieties of candies, and so many paths to choose from.

Each time the seeker steps through a particular door, they are going to learn something very valuable. And when they have learnt enough from that teacher, they leave and are ready to knock on the next door to continue with further education. Each door or pathway represents a steppingstone, and each stepping-stone eventually leads to self-realization. But this is not going to take place in one lifetime.

When the Higher Self enrolls the Soul Consciousness in the School of Earth, on average it will need to sign the Soul Consciousness up for between four hundred to six hundred reincarnations. (*Less, if you are a fast learner.*)

After your kundalini has risen and you have gained some of your God-like powers, it means that you will be able to speak directly to the Hierarchies, obtain astral travel and you will possess some healing powers, etc. This stage of your progress can be compared to the first day of the last year of graduation in university. Within this year you still have to study, and pass a number of exams. You can fail, and repeat the year again and again, or just finish on the first go with flying colors. After some time has passed, people will approach the recently awakened person, and request him/her to share their knowledge and wisdom with the rest of the seekers of knowledge. They quickly set up a place with the purpose of teaching those who are ready to learn from this "Master Teacher" who has risen to their God state, which is the highest qualification to gain amongst the rest of humanity. I would like to use a story as an example regarding the Master Teacher's journey.

The Pathway of the New Master Teacher or "Guru"

From this time forward he/she has to walk on a very special pathway. This pathway will test the new master teacher skill and wisdom. The pathway is made of honey and nectar, and its sweetness will draw all the flies and bees, and a variety of birds to itself constantly.

The pathway of honey: will represent to the people that this person has attained Self-realization and gained their Godhood-like abilities. The seekers of knowledge will flock to the "New Master Teacher" and request that they show them the easy way of self-realization. The new students will have the tendency to shower the teacher with adoration and respect. Regardless of the fact that the teacher never ask for all this adoration. **But** this is human nature and they will regard the teacher as God-like, and they will volunteer their free will, and be ready to follow the teacher's advice to the last letter. With time this type of adoration can make the Lower Ego rise again and the teacher can get drunk with all this adoration and self-importance. **But**, if the teacher has acquired enough mental strength and wisdom, then all this will not have any effect on them whatsoever.

The birds, flies and bees: represent the variety of people who will flock to the teacher. And the teacher has the responsibility to teach them according to their learning abilities and never harm them in any way. Some master teachers will teach with the highest respect, and enjoy helping those who are willing to learn. But you see this new master teacher is just that, a new teacher, which is the next level to gaining skill and since they are still living within the physical body, the Lower Ego still has the ability to test the young master teacher.

The Ancient Masters Give Us a Very Simple Guideline on How to Recognize a Good Teacher From a Bad One.

The fruit of their actions
Will reveal the type of teacher they happen to be

When a Teacher has abused their privileges toward their students, the time will come when the master teacher life cycle ends. The Soul Consciousness will not be exempt from further rebirth from the planet Earth School. This depends on how much damage has been done to others. When they are reborn again, they can lose all the privileges they gained when their Kundalini rose last time. In other words, they will still have to work hard once again, and one day they will walk on the testing pathway to Godhood once again.

The only doorway I would like to warn you about and draw your attention to, is one which offers guarantees to awaken the kundalini. That can usually happen before the kundalini is ready to do so. In India and unfortunately also around the world, there are a few ashrams (monasteries, schools) who will offer such services and promises. When people decide to join schools like this, and they do not check the schools and the teachers' credibility, this can be to the detriment of the student.

When the kundalini is forced through the chakras before it is ready, and reaches the crown chakra, the person will become mentally ill. No one will be able to heal them in this life cycle. And then it will take the person **seven lifetimes** before their mental health can be repaired.

Being a Palm Reader, I have read clients' palms that have a special marking that indicates that this person has experienced a mental disturbance in their recent past lives. But this time around, the person has a healthy mentality once again. During this type of reading I have always used caution on how to approach the client, and read for them, because they are still vulnerable and it would not take much to cause them mental confusion and possible harm. The simplest way to avoid any type of danger to yourself is to do the following: when you decide to learn and enroll in a class, first meditate or pray to your higher guidance to only guide you to the right teacher who will not cause you any harm and who will teach you with the highest integrity. When you ask you will be surprised when your request is fulfilled. The way you can tell that you are being guided by your spirit guides, is when you have a funny feeling that something is not right, your inner guide or instinct is signaling that you are at the wrong place, wrong class. If you don't listen to the warning, do not be surprised when things go wrong.

The Maintenance of the Four Bodies

There are seven Astral bodies around every physical form, which are also referred to as the seven layers of your auric field. Each one corresponds to its astral level of reality. The seven bodies are: the Physical, Emotional, Mental, Spiritual, Causal, Buddhic and Atmic body.

The Maintenance of the Four Bodies
You only need to work on the four bodies, and the last three upper bodies will also benefit from the work you do on the lower bodies.

The four bodies are: the Physical, Emotional, Mental and Spiritual.
Many guidelines and books have been written about how to progress safely on your spiritual journey. For example, learn to meditate, practice yoga and make sure that you work on the four body systems equally. If you just work on the spiritual body, and leave the physical behind, that will not aid you on your journey, but stagnate you. The physical body has to be maintained at all times.

Many spiritually aware people make the mistake of not paying enough attention and care for their physical body. That has resulted in a variety of illnesses. Any major illness and many minor ones can stop the kundalini from rising. *The Physical and the Spiritual Body Will Influence Each Other and Benefit from One Another.*

To Maintain the Physical body

- **Regular** daily exercise
- **Healthy** eating habits
- **No** drugs
- **No** regular drinking (alcohol)
- **Do** not push the body beyond its limits (*regarding overworking and not having enough sleep*)

The Spiritual Body Maintenance

- **Daily** meditation
- **Yoga**
- **Distant** healing to your loved ones and your enemies
- **Planet** earth healing

The Emotional and the Mental Body will
Influence Each Other
And Benefit from One Another.

The Emotional body

- **Knowing** the difference between right and wrong
- **Be** a student and stop being a martyr
- ***The Mental body* rational** thinking and evaluation
- **Stop** negative day dreaming
- **Take** charge and control of your thinking

6th CHAPTER

CONTENTS

- The Mind 88
- There Are Three Levels of Consciousness 89
- The Subconscious Mind, the Five Senses, and the Censor Zone 90
- The Power of Your Thoughts 94
- The Moon and its Eight Phases 95
- The Eight Phases of the Moon Chart 96
- Between the New Moon and the Full Moon 98
- How to Transform Old Negative Thought-Forms into a Radiant, Loving Light Meditation! 99
- How to Stop the Tendency to Daydream Negatively 100
- When You Are Confronted with a Negative Experience 102

The Mind and its Three Levels of Consciousness

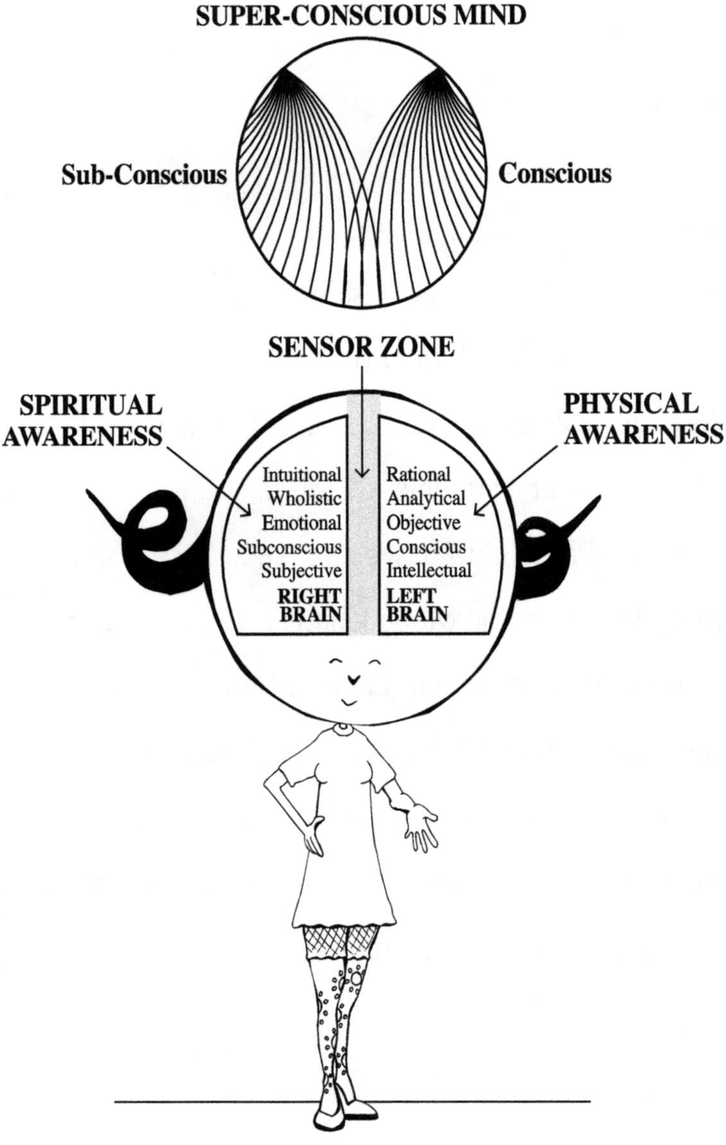

The Mind and its Three Levels of Consciousness

There Are Three Levels of Consciousness within the Mind
The Mind Takes Up Residence within the Eighth Chakra
Conscious, Subconscious, and the Super-Conscious Mind.

The Conscious Mind

Controls the Left Side of the Brain

1) Has the ability to analyze, and to be objective
2) Can intellectualize and is **Conscious** of everything at all times, 24 hours a day.

The Subconscious Mind,

Controls the Right Side of the Brain

1) Has the function to store everything, all your memories of this lifetime, and also everything before this lifetime and beyond.

2) Runs all of your Physical body functions 100%. Has no verbal language, only communicates through the Emotional, and Physical body by the sensing of pain, pleasure, fear, trauma, ill health, or being healthy, or when you feel happiness, or pride in your achievements.

3) The Subconscious Mind cannot reason!

The Super-Conscious Mind

Always in communication with the Higher Self and the Governing Hierarchy.

1) All knowing, and fully aware at all times.
2) Encases the human body in an oval-shaped energy field which is referred to as the "Auric Egg"

The Subconscious Mind, the Five Senses And the Censor Zone.

Through the five senses the Subconscious Mind receives information from the world around you as follows:

- with your **mouth**–taste,
- with your **hands**–touch,
- with your **ears**–hearing,
- with your **nose**–smell,
- and with your eyes–sight.

Through the Five Senses Everything Enters Into the Censor Zone First. The Censor Zone is a pathway that separates the two halves of the brain. This pathway is positioned between the right and the left side and is located on the top of your head. But before I explain the full function of the Censor Zone, I would like to tell you a story about a little boy's experience with a dog.

The story of the 5-year-old child and the strange, vicious, angry dog. This little boy is only 5 years old and his name is Harry. He has a puppy and they are the best of friends. They play together, trust and love one another at all times. But something happened to his dog and it disappeared from his life for good, and he now misses his dog very much.
One day Harry and his mum decided to go out to the park to play. In the park a new dog is running around, and Harry runs towards the dog, with the intention of playing with it. Not long ago, this dog had a very nasty experience, a group of children hurt it and now it does not trust any children. So, whenever the dog sees a child nearby it is ready to defend itself from them. So this angry dog, when noticing Harry, starts to runs towards him, and barks at him very angrily and gets ready to attack him at any moment. Harry was lucky because his mum saved him on this occasion. But it is too late; the emotion of fear has just been introduced to Harry, and registered as a danger in his subconscious mind.

This is the first time in Harry's life that he has experienced a trauma like this! He has just realized that not every dog is his friend! For the first time in his memory, fear and shock have registered about dogs, and this fear is then programmed into his Subconscious Mind, and the name of this new file is:

"BEWARE OF BARKING, KILLER DOGS!"

Next time Harry sees a dog on the street, he feels a tremendous fear that wells up inside his body. He starts crying and screaming, and of course the dog senses the little boy's fear, and gets into self-protection mode it starts barking and tries to attack the little boy. From now on, each time Harry sees any dog, the story will repeat itself.

What is happening in the Mind when a situation such as this is taking place? With your eyes you see the dog. The first piece of information enters into the censor zone.

1. Censor zone–registers the dog in the street or nearby.

2. Within the first second, the picture of the dog has entered through the eyes and begun to resonate for only one second in the censor zone; a doorway opens up in the Subconscious Mind (the store room) and claims this picture of the dog. It confirms that we have a full file registered on the dog scenario and that we are ready to press the "life-saving" alarm. Your Subconscious mind is ready to take charge, and gives orders to begin creating and producing fear chemicals that the dog can smell from long distances. The dog then translates your smell of fear, as danger to itself. So the dog then barks to let you know that it is afraid, but is ready to defend itself.

3. When the Emotional and Physical bodies **start to react with the emotion of fear**, you begin to scream at the top of your voice and the poor dog is barking its head off at you! The stage is set for an emotional time bomb!

By the way, *Harry has grown up now, and he is about six feet tall, and the dog is a little lapdog, which is barking very viciously at Harry from the other side of the road and Harry is reacting with a very familiar fear as always!* Harry has read about a seminar given about why dogs attack some people and not others. He decides to attend. **In the seminar this is what Harry learned:** If you have never experienced a negative fearful event before, and you only feel love and respect toward dogs, then they are usually very friendly towards you (most of them anyhow). Even the wisest dog can be handled especially when they feel your courage, strength and compassion. And if you send them pink light instead of fear the dog will be friendly towards you as well. The next time comes sooner than Harry would like, but he is ready as much as anyone can be. He will see a big dog, about 200m ahead, coming towards him. This is it! But this time, he is ready to face the dog, because he has now gained understanding and wisdom as to how to deal with this type of situation.

The Function of the Censor Zone and The Subconscious Mind.

As the picture of the dog enters your Censor Zone, it begins to resonate, and is waiting for the doorway to open up and make a claim for this information to be processed and to be put in the correct file.

In **your Subconscious Mind you have three types of recording cells**:

A–**The zero cell** is an empty cell, and is ready to record either way. The event will be put into the correct file each and every time!

B–**The negative cell** carries and records every fearful and painful event of your life. It stores and files each and every one according to its origin.

C–**The positive cell** carries and records every happy event in your life.
When Harry gained new information about how to deal with the dog, he gained a new recording in his Subconscious Mind, as an antidote against fear of the dog. Because of this new understanding about the dog and its

history, **the Conscious mind kicks in and starts to reason!** It claims the right to the vision of the dog in the Censor Zone, and demands that all the files on the fearful dog history should be wiped out, and be replaced with a new program of behavior.

The antidote is: visualizing a pink light in the center of your heart chakra and then expanding this pink light throughout your body, out into your Aura, and towards the supposedly vicious little dog. And sending a message with the pink light says something to the effect of, "I am not afraid of you anymore, I would like to be your friend". The dog will walk up to you and allow you to pat its head. You realize the fear that you had before has disappeared and a new confidence and trust has taken its place.

When the Subconscious Mind dealt with the picture of the dog before, it was on its own, so it reacted in the only way it knew how; by alerting the fear chemicals, which in turn activated your survival mechanism, and then you were ready to run for cover.

The Conscious Mind had never been given a chance to step in and deal with the situation. So it had no choice but to stand aside and watch the scenario play out.

The Super-Conscious Mind will not step in to stop the calamity either. Only when the Conscious Mind steps in to reason the situation out, can the Super-Conscious Mind bring in divine wisdom. This appears in the form of love, compassion, deeper understanding, forgiveness and the realization that it is only a lesson. This is the first time in this matter that the three levels of Consciousness of the Mind are realigned and in balance, and working in harmony with one another. In this case the lesson has been learnt and wisdom has been gained.

That is why the old saying goes, *Count to 10 before you reply to any argument or verbal assault.*

When you count to 10 you give the Conscious Mind a chance to step in and reason, instead of allowing the Subconscious Mind to react. Each time

you react in any given situation, the scenario will be repeated over and over again, until the lesson has been replaced by a positive attitude in any situation. Your destiny on this Planet is to learn how to bring harmony and balance between the three levels of Consciousness of the Mind, and not to use them independently. When you display negative thoughts and behaviors, you hurt others, and yourself.
I call this, learning the hard way!

The Power of Your Thoughts.

The Conscious Mind thinks and works constantly throughout the day. It never stops day after day. The Conscious Mind thinks consciously, and controls subconsciously at all Times.

Everything is made of energy! Each thought-form is a living, conscious energy! You are the creator of each thought-form you will ever think of! Because of this ability the saying goes:

"*Whatever you think and whatever you believe, will be* **manifested** *into your reality!"*

Each and every negative thought that has been created by you that has not been transformed into positive thoughts will be stored within the fourth layer of your auric field. This fourth layer is called the **Astral Auric** body. The negative thought forms appear in your Aura like small patches of dark clouds.

Negative thought-forms
And their destructive power in our daily life.

These negative dark clouds when held within your auric field have been influencing and affecting your decision-making abilities (as if this negativity has its own life, strength and intelligence). Accordingly, this dark energy will draw situations and people into our daily lives to act out that situation. And that is the reason the saying goes, "like attracts like".

The Moon and its Eight Phases

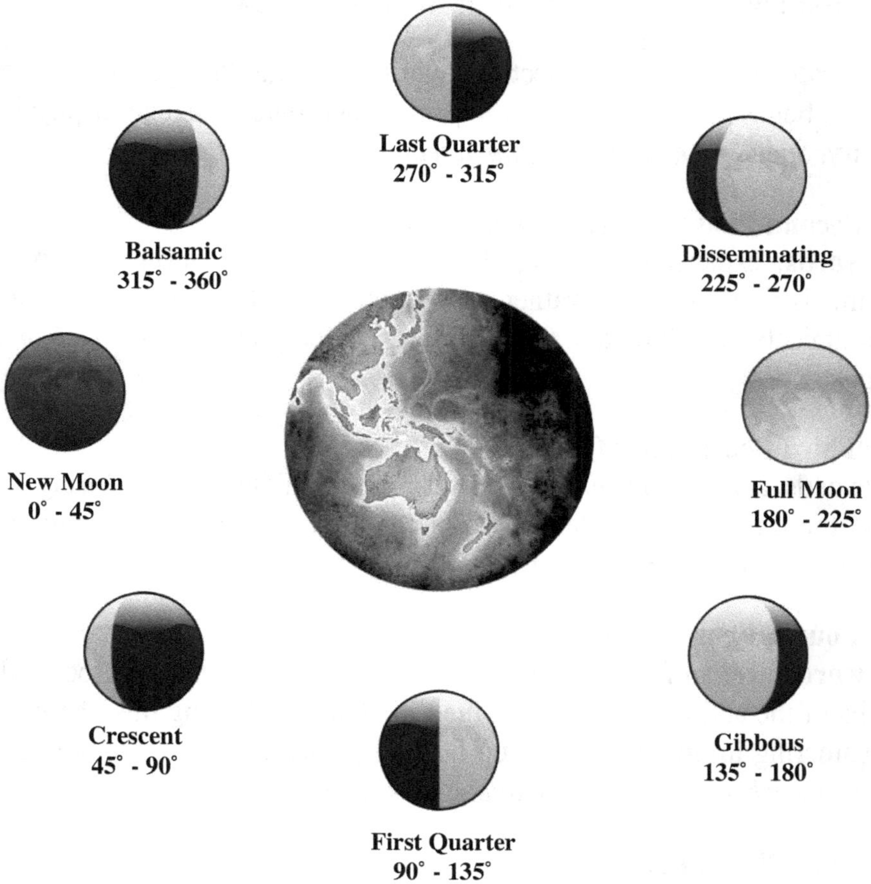

The Moon being the closest to Planet Earth controls the rhythm of the sea and all its creatures. It also governs the flow of blood in the humans and their emotional body. Each night the Moon gives off a different amount of light according to its changing relationship with the Sun. Within a **twenty–eight** day cycle the Moon will have passed through **eight phases**, each phase lasting three and a half days.

The Eight Phases of the Moon Chart

The First Phase: New Moon–the beginning of a new cycle.

Keywords: beginnings, projection, clarity. During this phase the new cycle is being seeded by your vision, inner and outer. Engage in physical activity. *Spend time alone and plan ahead.*

The Second Phase: Crescent phase
Keywords: expansion, growth, struggle, opportunity. During this phase the time is right for you to gather the wisdom learned in the new phase and communicate your intention to move forward. *Listen and Absorb. Commit to your goal.*

The Third Phase: First Quarter
Keywords are: action, expression, growth, breaking away. During this phase the time is right to take action to achieve your goals by expressing your needs and desires. *Act now.*

The Fourth Phase: Gibbous
Keywords are: analyze, prepare, and trust. This is the time to process the results of the actions taken during the First Quarter. During this phase you are gathering information. Give up making judgments; it will only lead to worry. *Your knowledge is incomplete, look within.*

The Fifth Phase: Full Moon
Keywords are: fulfillment, illumination, realization, experience. You are given a clear view so that you can make adjustments to put you back on track for manifesting the goals you set at the new phase. *Go to a public place. Do something with a friend, understand others.*

The Sixth Phase: Disseminating
Keywords are: demonstration, distribution, sharing and introspection to further and process your advancement toward your goal by looking at the results of your adjusting actions taken at the Full phase. During this phase

you gain clarity by sharing what you've learned through awareness. *Demonstrate your power of abundance by giving back to your community.*

The Seventh Phase: Quarter

Keywords are: realignment, revision, integration, cleansing.

This is the time to take closing action, to follow-up and complete the activities begun at the New Phase.

During this phase you become aware of what is and is not working with respect to the achievement of your goal for the cycle. The movement is toward integration.

Open to your success. Manifest your goals, and be responsible

The Eight Phase: Balsamic

The end of one cycle and the beginning of another.

Keywords are: transition, release, transformation, renewal, you must let go of everything you have been working on that does not deal with current cycle issues. During this phase you reflect on the passing cycle and prepare for the new. Trust in renewal. It is important to separate from others now so that you can clear the intellect of negativity.

When Negative Thought-Forms or Daydreaming Enter Your Mind Between the New Moon and the Full Moon.

I would like to use the golden circle as an example of a pathway between the New Moon and the Full Moon.

The Golden Pathway

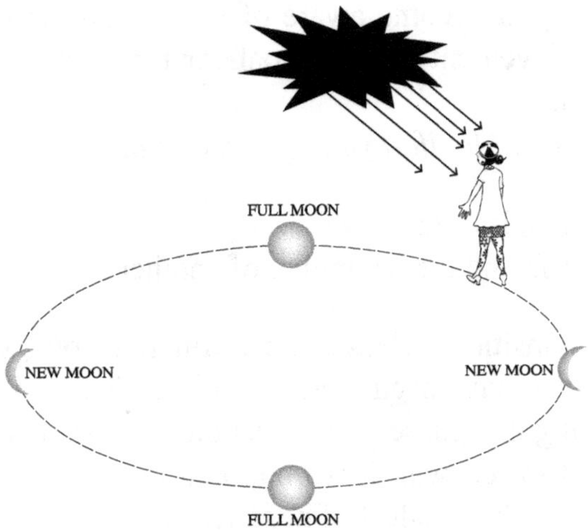

Imagine a large golden circle lies on the ground just a few meters distance. Directly above the circle a few meters high two small bowls of light will appear. One of the bowls of light will position itself on the left side of the circle and will represent the new Moon. The second bowl of light will position itself on the right side of the circle and will represent the full Moon.

Let's begin our journey, by stepping on the golden pathway under the New Moon and as we begin to walk away from the new Moon. Suddenly a negative memory appears in your mind from nowhere (you may think) and if you allow this negative memory to occupy your mind more than one minute, and continue for more than 10 minutes, you realize that you don't want to think about that negative situation any more, and begin to think of a more positive subject. But 15 minutes has passed from the last time you finished with that negative scenario, and you realize it's back again and you are creating new strategies around it. You do not know how to put a stop to this nightmare. It feels like this negative issue has full control over your thinking and willpower.

You will be haunted by this horrible nightmare, which is playing in your mind. This will continue for about three and half days, and then suddenly it will stop. And in the meantime the dark cloud has doubled its size, and is patiently waiting for the next month to begin once again.

How did this event occur?

Because there was a small, darkish cloud in your Aura, when you began to walk away from the New Moon three days later, you reached that dark cloud and you walked right under it. The cloud that contains the negative "memory story" will first shoot a dark tentacle down towards you which will then attach itself to you. When the first memory of thought registers in your consciousness, and if you allow it to continue for more than one minute, it will then take a stronger hold within your consciousness and direct the negative story until the allocated time has passed. In the meantime, the perimeter of that cloud has doubled in size and strength. Each month when you set out on your golden circle of journey, you will have to walk beneath this cloud. This negative cloud will play with your mind by being able to take control and test your intellect and will power.
The negative thought-form behaves like it has a remote control to your will power, and it will play with your will power, to its heart's content. One day, when you have had enough, you will meet someone who has learned how to deal with this type of negative thinking and they will be happy to share this recipe with you.

How to Transform Old Negative Thought-Forms Into a Radiant, Loving Light Meditation!

When an old negative memory enters your mind, you will recognize its intent by now. Stop whatever you may be doing, and take charge by focusing your full attention on this thought-form and nothing else!

Visualize in your mind's eye that you are walking on the golden circle, and you are standing right under this dark cloud. Imagine and visualize that from your heart chakra, a silvery pink light beam of energy is pouring through into your arms. Raise your arms, open them and turn your palms towards that dark cloud, then encase and trap that dark cloud in a silvery pink light cocoon.- **Then** you can drop your arms to your side and allow the rest of the silvery pink light to expand throughout your entire body. As the dark cloud has been cocooned in a silvery pink light, you are now ready to address yourself to that story of darkness, by talking to it as if it were a living person,–**My dear Emotional Body**, thank you for keeping and looking after this painful experience of my life. It has taught me a lot about myself and the people who played out this story with me. But, now I am ready to take control of this emotion and to transform this pain of dark energy" into a positive, loving light. In the meantime, as you talk to this cloud of darkness you will witness the silvery light eating up the darkness rapidly.–**Keep talking** to it lovingly and enforce the transformation as the silvery and pink light gains a bigger territory by each passing second and transforms the dark into the light. Almost immediately, the darkness is completely transformed into a pink radiant light. Peace and harmony will expand through your whole being.

You may find yourself doing this type of negative thought-form clearing very often and regularly. It may take a short time or it may take a bit longer than you expected. And very soon you will realize that your mind has less and less desire to dwell on negative issues.

How to Stop the Tendency to Daydream Negatively.

Please remember when you think negative thoughts, this will stay within your Aura and will set the space and rhythms of your life! It will draw people into your daily life that has the same problems as you, to play this scenario out and learn from this. This will continue until you have had enough and are ready to turn it around completely.

How do you deal with negative thinking?

From the moment you realize that you have been thinking a negative thought, you have one second to say, **CANCEL this now!** Then visualize that what you have been thinking so far is captured on a big blackboard. **Then** visualize a silver patch of light appearing, which will then erase that story right off the big blackboard.

After the story has been erased that particular story will never have a chance to take up residence in your auric field and to become a negative driving force in your consciousness in the future. It takes a lot of hard work, but in the end you will be the winner.

As the saying goes: *If you want to change your world for the better, YOU have to change your thinking!*
Because your thoughts and actions will shape your future and its possibilities.

How to Gain a Higher Understanding & Perspective When You Are Confronted With a Negative Experience.

This exercise should take place in the form of writing.
Imagine that you have been summoned to the high court. Judgment will be passed on the issue that has just occurred recently. When you step into the courtroom you will find to your amazement that it looks very different from any other courtroom you have ever seen before. The room is segmented into four quarters and each quarter will be represented by a particular color:

- The first section is in the color **red**
- The second section is in the color **orange**
- The third section is in the color **green**
- The fourth section is in the color **blue**

In the middle of the room resides a large circle, this is where the judges are seated. This circle appears in two colors: gold and ice pink. The three judges have already taken their seats in the middle of the circle. The Judges are your own Conscious, Subconscious and Super Conscious Mind.

Within each section there is only one chair with a small writing desk. You are wearing a robe that emanates the colors of the rainbow at all times. You will present this case in four levels of understanding to the judges. When you take a seat in the first section you will take up the color and personalities of this section and only speak of what has been allocated to this section to talk (write) about and nothing more or less.

The 1st section is red–write down the situation as it has taken place without any blame or finger pointing at this stage.

For example: *so and so came in to work very angry and told you off.*
When you have finished writing your report, just stand up and walk into the next section of the courtroom.

The 2nd section is orange–Describe how this attack made you feel.

For example: *I felt like crawling under the carpet, I felt so embarrassed that everyone at work was staring at me as if I had robbed a bank or something. Yes, yesterday I did do some of the things he accused me of but I am not the only one who made a mistake and this person told me to do it that way in the first place, obviously I misunderstood the instructions he gave me.*

The 3rd section is green–Put yourself in their shoes. Why do you think this person behaved like this and what made them lose their grip on reality?

The 4th section is blue–If this situation happened to your best friend, what sort of advice would you be giving them to deal with the situation?
The four steps of review will help you to see, to comprehend and allow you to change your opinion about the experience and be able to see the situation for the first time as a lesson and not as a victim of circumstance.

What have you learned from this exercise?
If you use this type of exercise after each painful event, in time this will help you to develop a different perspective and better understanding like you have never done before. Your relationships with people in general will improve tremendously. And when you are ready to send a silent blessing to those people who have played out this event with you, you know for sure that you have progressed forward on your journey. Have you realized that without them you would not be able to gain the experience and gain the knowledge to better yourself? After all it is not the end of the world; it is only a game, the game of life.

The Soul, as the Silent Witness and Guardian
Until you are ready to know and learn about your true identity as a Soul Consciousness, your Soul will communicate to you via the Subconscious Mind and activates certain feelings within you. Sometimes we call these gut feelings or warning bells.

Example: When your **Soul Consciousness** wants to get your attention and warn you against any danger that you may be facing at that point in time, a warning feeling or happy excitement will be felt within your solar plexus (*at the upper part of your tummy region*), or within the middle of your chest, which we also refer to as the Heart Chakra. Either way, whenever you disregard this warning, you will pay for it by getting a wrong deal, or missing out on a lifetime of opportunities. The more often you listen to and rely on your inner guidance and trust its wisdom, the more your life will progress positively, and you will then be able to identify more with the real self, and not with the emotional body and its negative belief systems. In order to understand yourself and the world around you, you need to understand and recognize the functions of the three levels of Consciousness of your Mind, how they work, and how they apply to you on a day-to-day basis.

When the Soul Consciousness is Able to Manifest and Take Charge of the Situation. Picture this: You just happen to be walking down the street, and you notice that a middle-aged lady is sitting on a bench. There is nothing unusual about that, but something about her just does not seem right to you. You even walk away for a short distance and **a nagging feeling manifests in your Solar plexus**. You turn around and approach this lady. You express your concern about her, and ask her if you can assist her in some manner. The lady turns towards you and confides in you, that just five minutes ago someone snatched her handbag. Now she cannot open her car, because her keys were in the bag, she has no money to call anyone for help. Also, she cannot do her food shopping and has no food in her kitchen to cook for her family. She looks devastated. **Without thinking**, you offer to take her to the police station, because your car is just parked a few meters away. As you drive her to the next police station, you also offer your mobile phone for her to call a family member for help. When you arrive at the police station you go in with her and give your part of the story to the police officer. You then offer the lady $100 as a gift to give her a bit of a start. You then realize that you need to go because you are already one hour late for a very important meeting you are supposed to attend. As you sit in your car ready to drive away, you realize you completely forgot about yourself and without thinking about the important meeting that you needed to attend, **you allowed yourself to aid another person in need**.

When you help someone who may be in need, without thinking you just jump in and rescue or aid that person without thinking of what the consequences will be for you. After the task has been fulfilled and you sit down and realize what has just taken place, you will experience in your heart chakra the most exquisite feeling of love and grace that expands throughout your entire being. Nothing can match this feeling of divine peace and harmony that you feel at that moment.

Alternatively, you may also express yourself through art with painting, handicraft, or by writing a book, poetry, playing or writing music, or any other aspect you may fulfill on the Spiritual path, as a healer, tarot and palm reader. This is a service to humanity from the heart without any strings attached. That is the time when your Soul consciousness is working through you. Usually this beautiful feeling is letting you know when you're allowing the Soul to manifest and take action.

7th CHAPTER

CONTENTS

- Personal and Family Karmic Inheritances 108
- Karma Sharing Within the Four Family Circles 109
- The Character Roles Played Within the First Family Circle 110
- Personality and Family Karma 110
- When the Truth Will Set You Free 111
- The Second Stage of Your Karmic Relationship 112
- Can Anyone Read the Journey of Your Life? 115

Personal and Family Karmic Inheritances

The Story of the Relay Team in Swimming
The Family reincarnation cycle is very intricate and complicated to explain in a few words. To make this information as easy as possible to understand, I will compare it to a sport team in a swimming competition. This particular swimming team consists of four athletes and they are referred to as the relay team. Each swimmer will have a different style of swimming such as breaststroke, butterfly, backstroke and freestyle. Each of those swimmers will be the very best in their country, and this is the reason they have been selected to be part of the relay team and represent their country at the Olympic Games. When one person jumps into the water to swim the length of the pool and they are about to finish, the swimmer will need to touch the bell at the finishing line. Only then can the next person in line jump into the water and swim. You will find that each individual swimmer will have a different score, some will gain higher marks, and some will have lower marks. The important thing is the judges will add up all the four individual athletes' score and that final number can earn each athlete the bronze, silver or gold medal at the Olympic Games.

Now you have some idea how the relay team works, let's transfer this analogy into the family reincarnation cycle.

The difference is that in the family relay team, when someone finishes their life cycle and passes over, the next member of the family will then arrive as a newborn. The newborn is ready to continue to improve upon any particular subject that the last person was working on before they passed on. The newborn will possess higher knowledge and the know-how and ability to progress to the next level regarding that particular subject.

When the Soul Consciousness Gains Experience And Knowledge.

Remember we have seven levels of consciousness to work with and improve upon throughout our many life cycles. Each time we are reborn we have a chance to progress forward or take a few steps back which will provide you with more learning and gain more understanding regarding that particular subject. This is the main reason that on average the Soul Consciousness needs to reincarnate between 400-600 lifetimes before it is ready to graduate from the planet earth school of learning.

The Seven Major Subjects That the Soul Consciousness Needs to Excel in are:

- **Physical body**–to keep it healthy and in harmony at all times
- **Emotional body**–turning negative thought forms into positive, and think before you react.
- **Creativity**–learning about love and respect for self and others
- **Causal**–mind your language, because the power of your words acts as a weapon to heal or to kill
- **Spiritual**–realization of the Self as the Spirit and not the body
- **Mental**–learn to use reasoning and think before you react

Karma Sharing Within the Four Family Circles

Each time you are reborn you will be interacting and **role-playing** with each individual member within the four family circles.

The first family circle represents: Grandparents, from both sides of the family, uncles, aunties, and cousins.

The second family circle represents your immediate family members such as: your mum, dad, your sisters and brothers, if you have any.

The third family circle represents: boy/girl friends, spouses, and your own children.

The fourth circle represents: your close friends and enemies, teachers, work colleagues.

The Character Roles Played Within the First Family Circle

When you are born into a family circle you will eventually be going to play all those character roles.

The character roles are:

The 1st role: you will begin as a child to your mother and father
The 2nd role: you are a grandchild to your grandparents
The 3rd role: you are a sibling to your sisters/brothers, if you have any
The 4th role: you are a niece/nephew to your aunties and uncles
The 5th role: you are a cousin to your aunties' and uncles' children

Let's presume that the first family circle consists of fifty people. That will indicate that all the five roles will be played out fifty times, and when each individual reaches that particular time to become a grandparent, each and every one will have the chance to improve on being the grandparent.
Because of that one step forward progress earned by one person suddenly all other 49 players receive a better understanding of how to become a better grandfather. Just think of it as a family bank account. When one family member puts money into that account the other members of the family will all be able to have more money in their account.

Personal and Family Karma

What is Karma? Cause and effect–for each action there is an equal and opposite reaction. Your present circumstances are the product of previous actions, and what you do today will affect what happens tomorrow. A blueprint will be devised for each individual's Soul Consciousness based upon the latest results of previous life grades. When the family has been selected for the Soul Consciousness to be born into, every member within that family circle will be compatible with one another. And the role playing and reverse role-playing will begin once again.

Mothers and fathers from the time of birth will be connected from their heart chakra to the newborn heart chakra with the energy cord that consists of "unconditional love." This bond will teach parents and children alike the lessons of what unconditional love is like.

When you are playing the role of the child:
You will experience what it is like to be loved unconditionally by your parents. For instance, when your parents make you feel that you are safe and protected from the world, and assure you that you are perfect and you can achieve anything you want to. And later on, for some reason, when everyone else gives up on you, your parents will not. They will always stand by you, love and protect you until their last moment spent on planet earth. And when occasionally you gain an archenemy throughout many life cycles, the only way to change the "hate, mistrust and the thirst to kill one another", is by stepping into the role of the mother and child. Many times you may have to play this character role, and only the unconditional love of the mothers or fathers can heal the deadly "hate and mistrust" that has accumulated throughout the ages.

When the Truth Will Set You Free

As a Palm and Tarot reader, I have seen many clients with this type of karmically linked parent-child relationship. So, when I explain to them that this "caustic relationship" stretches back through many past lives and in this present life they have the privilege to be able to change and sort out their problems. The thing is that they cannot run away from it and it is up to each party to learn and communicate with one another to change this recurring emotional battle. After they receive this information they usually look relieved, as if a ton of bricks has just been lifted from their shoulders.
Your immediate family members will present the most important lessons you need to gain passing marks. When you are grown up and you find that you are not getting along with your parents, the easiest thing you can do is to put as much distance between yourself and them. If anyone asks about your parents you will talk about them as if they are the worst people in the world. And when you make poor choices, and make many mistakes, you will blame your parents because when you were young they failed to live

up to your expectations. With this type of attitude and thinking you are giving yourself a license to keep repeating all your negative attributes forever to your heart's content. And with an attitude such as this you will behave and act like a "Martyr".

But if you take a stand as a "student" and approach your parents with the intent to understand and work things out, you and your parents can progress in leaps and bounds.

The ancient wise ones stated that: *you can get rid of your friends, but you cannot get rid of your parents. They are yours to keep for the rest of your life.*

They are your first and most important teachers in your life. If you cannot get along with them, and are unable to work out your differences, your relationships with others will also suffer and your progress will be very slow.

The second stage of your karmic relationships

This is when you begin to date boy/girlfriends and eventually select a spouse. All those people will present a past life karmic relationship. This can be both a positive or negative kind and it depends upon your karmic inheritance. When you attract negative relationships into your life it usually signifies that you are lacking knowledge regarding "**self respect** and the ability to give respect to others." This is then combined with the lack of knowledge on how to negotiate and meet each other half way. When you have problems like this, you need to stop and look back at your family background. You may not realize at this point in time that you yourself have inherited each and every one of those negative behavior patterns that you are accusing your parents of. And when it's your turn to enter into relationships you will behave just like your parents used to behave, and in some cases you will behave even worse than your parents ever did.

Then one day, when you are ready to take responsibility for your actions and finally realize that you deserve better you will move out of that self-destructive relationship for good, and this new realization will set you free. You just earned yourself one step forward on the evolutionary path. In other words, you have graduated from being a martyr and a doormat, and you have become a student of life.

The Student's Way of Dealing with Negative Issues

The students of the planet earth school of learning become aware of the simple fact that so **many things** out there that we do not know of, or understand, or even aware about–actually do exist. And the only way to find out and learn about these things is by asking questions all the time.
When we face any negative situations in our daily lives we can approach this issue in either of two ways: the Martyr's way or the Student's way.

The Martyr's way will ask–"But why me?"
The student on the other hand will ask: "What are you trying to teach me, what I need to look at to gain more understanding regarding this issue?" The process for working out any negative situation will proceed in two stages.

The first stage will take place in the mental plane, for instance, every time a thought form pops up in your mind regarding that issue, the first rule is to not allow your mind to make up excuses on your behalf **but** to instantly confront that thought form with these questions:

"*What are you trying to teach me, and why? I don't understand the significance of this lesson.*"

Sometimes you may have to ask those questions over and over, and it may take a whole week before you receive any clarity and understanding of the situation. But perseverance will gift you with a clear view of comprehension. And you will realize that sometimes the crux of the problem began long before in many past lives. **For example**: the son may be accusing his father of chasing every potential partner away, with his endless interfering attitude. So he asks his father to stay away from him and his lady friends. The poor father is scratching his head, because according to him and also everyone around him, he always behaves with courtesy and respect towards all the girls the son has introduced to the family. He cannot understand why his son is accusing him with this type of behavior.

In this life cycle the father's behavior belongs in the student's category. And he has spent long hours thinking about why his son has been accusing him with this type of attitude. During his meditation he finally receives a past life vision. He was shown that in that particular life he was the mother of his present son. The mother chased all the women out of his son's life. She was very domineering and ruled with iron fists. Her son on the other hand lived a very lonely and angry life because of her. So the son promised himself next time around he would guard his personal relationships with an iron fist. **But** let's just take one more step back into another past life and see why this mother guarded her son and could not bear to see him happy with anyone. In the earlier past life the mother was playing the role of his wife and the present son was the husband. At the beginning of their marriage the wife was very loving and trusting. She did not realize that she had married the biggest womanizer and loser in the region. In a very short space of time they began to have children one after the other. In those days divorce was out of the question. So she had to grin and bear it, and she promised herself no man was ever going to use her and shame her as this husband did.

So you see, no-one is as innocent as sometimes we perceive. We must never judge before we really know all the facts. In this life cycle new character roles have taken place, and this time around the one who used to be his mother, has taken the role of the father. They have come together in this life cycle with the purpose that they have to heal their lost love, and rebuild trust and respect towards one another. When the father comes out of his meditation he will have a deeper understanding of the present situation. He will not be taking the accusation of his son personally, because that behavior he is accusing him of now is **not applicable** this time around. He has already transformed that negative behavior that has taken him four separate life cycles do so with other study partners. He gained enough wisdom, and he will be able to heal the past mistakes with his son this time around. The next time when he is going to meet up with his son, he will share his past life vision and assure him that this time around he will not behave as he did in that particular past life. Because of this realization–*The truth will set them free*. The son and father will finally have the chance to rebuild trust and love back into their relationship. When we engage in a verbal misunderstanding and fight with anyone, neither party is going to be happy. Deep down everyone wants to work out the situation, and when one of the opponents offers a green olive branch most of the time it will be accepted gratefully.

Can Anyone Read the Journey of Your Life?

Nowadays it is very easy to find and select a reputable Astrologer or Palm reader who may possess the ability to read your blueprint. **But** I must warn you that each Astrologer or Palm reader will give you readings according to their ability. It is very important when you decide to select a reader, to make sure the person whom you choose is on your level of understanding, otherwise you may walk away disappointed. Your inner feelings of guidance will always give you an indication of whether that person is right or wrong for you.

The Astrologer will cast your birth chart (blueprint) based upon your time of birth, date and location. Your full itinerary of this Earthly life will be laid out within each house, and the planets are distributed around the 12 house system. This will determine the general shape of your personality structure. **Within the zodiacs** a variety of alignments signify the present which is based upon **your past lives** and the **near future** that is about to unfold. It will also indicate if and when you will have an easy or hard time which you must learn from, or use their potential this time around.

An Astrologer can also provide you with relationship charts. Like for instance who you share positive or negative karmic patterns with. People such as your parents, potential relationships, spouse, children, and work related business relationships and basically anyone who can provide you with the time of birth date of birth, and location. Without this information your chart cannot be as accurate as it should be when you have all the correct data.

In Palm Reading: Please remember every Palm reader will have different abilities and will do readings for you accordingly. When I do Palm readings I am able to read the full itinerary of your **present, past** and **future** possibilities. Your palms may hold positive and negative situations, but every negative situation also has its antidote and if you are wise enough and willing to work hard, you will be able to turn your life around for the better. I believe the reason we are on Planet Earth is to do just that.

8th CHAPTER

CONTENTS

- The Martyr's Pathway...118
- When the Three Major Attributes Become the Currency of Your Life...120
- The Self-Righteous Lower Ego Driven Individual....................121
- The Beginning of Low Self-Esteem, Self-Love Value and Respect...122

The Martyr's Pathways

The Definition of the Phrase: "Being a Martyr"

From Wikipedia, the free encyclopedia:

Martyr: One who will choose to make great sacrifices to further one's belief, or a cause or principle.

One who makes a great show of suffering because of misfortune or hardship in life in order to arouse sympathy.

Or when someone has not developed enough courage and self-respect to step out of the rut they find themselves in.

The Martyr's Pathways
Throughout our many life cycles we all play the role of the Martyr or the Student to a certain degree. But some of us play it more than others and someone with this type of attitude will stand out more amongst others. The sad part is that those people don't even realize how much they are living their lives as a Martyr. But before we condemn this character trait, I would like to remind you that in order to learn we must perfect the three main character traits within ourselves, which are:

- **Love**–for self and others,
- **Respect**–for self and others,
- **Courage**–to stand up for yourself and what you believe in.

Without perfecting these three main character traits, the student cannot graduate from the Planet Earth School of Learning. Each and every one of us will have to walk on this road. I refer to this road as "The Martyr's Highway". The purpose of this highway is to supply you with all the experiences you need in order to understand and acknowledge the difference whenever you experience emotional and physical pain that has been knowingly and willingly inflicted upon you by other people.

Or when you are in the reverse situation, when you are placed in the opposite position and you find yourself inflicting emotional pain and abuse on another person, you need to know whether you will be able to stop in time and treat them better than you have been treated, or release your anger and frustrations on them.

When you are able to stand up for yourself, or in reverse, when you are able to choose to stop inflicting pain upon others for the very first time, you will be able to progress forward positively from that moment onward.

But first let's see how someone needs to behave to be called a Martyr.

The Martyr's attributes:

- Everyone's fault, but theirs
- Nobody loves them
- Nobody respects them
- They do not believe that they deserve to be happy

If you ask them whether they love themselves or if they have any positive attributes the answer for both of those questions is always **NO**.

When this type of person finds themselves in a negative situation, they firmly believe it was **the other person's fault**, and they had no choice but to behave as they did.

As Dr Phil states in his very successful TV show "You cannot change what you do not acknowledge". And **I agree!**

The Martyr has no self-respect or self-love to speak of. When someone is lacking these vital character traits, they have the tendency to settle for second best in relationships or anything that life offers in general.

When the Three Major Attributes Become The Currency in Your Life.

- **Love**–for self and others
- **Respect**–for self and others
- **Courage**–to stand up for your beliefs and accept new challenges in life

These three main attributes will become the major currencies in your life when you are born onto Planet Earth. Over time you will learn and understand the value of these three important character traits. The more you advance in this understanding, the more your life accomplishments will grow. Everyone that you are ever going to meet in your life will be your teacher in one form or another, and they will be teaching these important subjects and testing you constantly throughout your life.

Backgrounds and circumstances may affect who we are.
But ultimately we are responsible for who we become.

All the Teachers (*as your study partners throughout your life*) will be Divided into Three Main Groups:

The 1st group includes those who have already gained a higher wisdom of these three subjects, and they behave and conduct their everyday life with high integrity. Everyone treats them with respect, and people seek them out for advice and leadership. Their behavior and attitude is a beacon of light for others to see, and they give us hope that this level of wisdom can be achieved by anyone.

This group will be presented to you as possibly one or both of your parents, teachers, family members, friends or anyone who possesses the wisdom of those three attributes.

The 2nd group will be able to push you beyond your limit of endurance. **It will be presented to you as** your archenemies and those who have the tendency and ability to push your buttons with ease and make your life a living hell on Earth.

The 3rd group will lend you a shoulder to cry on when you need it the most. **They will be presented to you** as your best friends or anyone who has compassion and cares to listen and to console you in times of need.

The Self-Righteous–Lower Ego Driven Individual
This person will be your most valuable teacher. And their job is to supply you with painful experiences on the subjects of **self-value, self-love and self-respect**. This self-righteous teacher has no patience, is extremely critical and demands that you always do things with perfection regardless of whether or not they are capable of doing it themselves. This person has the skill to use their words as weapons, and when it suits them they are able to cut you into pieces in seconds with their words and reduce your self-esteem and self-value to nothing. If you are unable to stand up for yourself or to protect yourself because of your age, or simply because no-one is around to defend you from this nasty person, within a short space of time this individual will take your willpower and self-respect, and turn it into **self-doubt and fear**.

The Types of Situations That Can Cause Self-Doubt to Set In.

Usually when someone constantly criticizes what you do and how you do it. **If anyone** asks them why they are constantly criticizing you, they will answer that they are trying to teach you to become a better person. They firmly believe this harsh treatment is in your own best interest and according to them; this is the right way to go about it. They never give you any guidance or encouragement in the subject or issue you are currently dealing with.

These types of teachers are also lacking in wisdom and patience, compassion and also the art of teaching.

They always demand perfect results from the very first attempt you ever make at anything. They have not yet realized that there is no such thing as perfection. The reason for that is because everything is constantly changing and evolving. **If, by any chance**, you manage to do something right by them, instead of approval the best you will have as a response is "it's about time", or "you have been lucky this time".

The Beginning of Low Self-Esteem When you are constantly subjected to criticisms this will register into your subconscious mind, and very soon you begin to think and believe that, "I am nothing but a loser", or "*I am incompetent*", **or** "*I am not very smart*". Then you begin to compare yourself to others who are more capable than you are.

This type of personal evaluation will result in low self-esteem. It will limit your opportunities and will give you an excuse not to try as hard as you should or normally would. As a result, you may end up creating self-fulfilling prophecies for your future possibilities. Remember: whatever you believe about yourself is what you will draw into your life, and those situations will certainly verify that you are good for nothing and that you are a loser and incapable of achieving more.

When you change your thinking and your belief systems, you will be able to change your possibilities in life accordingly.

Self Love, Value and Respect .*Developing Self Love, Value and Respect is a Lifelong Challenge. And it takes Many Lifetimes to Perfect.*

The people in our lives act as mirrors in this process. They give us attention and encouragement; we see positive images of ourselves. At other times, our interactions with others may make us feel unattractive, incompetent or even invisible.

Self-respect is at the heart of respecting others. When you can identify and appreciate your strengths and accept your vulnerabilities, it's easier to truly respect the value in others.

Mistakes are positive, not negative. You shouldn't go out of your way to make them, but when they happen, you learn from that situation, forgive yourself and go forward.

We respect people who have traits we admire. As young children we begin to respect things we see in the adults who are present in our lives both good and bad. What a child respects is determined in large part by what they are exposed to. If they are raised in antisocial homes they may grow up to actually respect and admire antisocial acts. They aspire to be just like mom and dad.

In schools, children see how their teachers solve problems and cope with challenges. If their teachers handle conflicts by listening, thinking and staying calm then the children come to respect and mirror these behaviors.

Being humble means that you do not brag about you or put yourself above others.

Humility is a characteristic that is prized throughout the ancient times. Humility means that you are caring and unselfish. You may have the principle to always tell the truth. But if you go around lying to people, you will not have a respectful character. If someone says that you are acting like a martyr, you are NOT just doing something nice for others. Evidently you are making sure they know you are doing something nice and/or putting yourself out for them. The question is how do you behave towards others–with respect or disrespect? If you behave with disrespect you are still learning the hard way and you belong in the category of the Martyrs.

But if you behave with respect towards others, you have learned and gained wisdom on this subject and you have been upgraded to the students' category. *Self-Respect* ***needs*** *to be Developed and Earned*

Having Self-Respect Means That You Value Yourself as a Person

It does not mean that you are arrogant or conceited. Stop undermining your worth by comparing yourself with others because we are all different, and everyone is special and unique in their own way. The amount of respect you have for yourself will determine the amount of respect you command from others.

Courage

Don't be Afraid to Encounter Risks.
It is by taking chances that we learn and gain knowledge in life.

Letting others know how you think and feel doesn't have to be confrontational or aggressive, but it does involve **taking a stand for yourself** and be responsible for your failures. Failure comes about by not paying enough attention to what you are doing and ignoring the feedback your world is constantly giving you.

9th CHAPTER

CONTENTS

- ◆ Meditation and Prayers 126
- ◆ A Variety of Meditations to Choose From 127
- ◆ How to Prepare Yourself for Meditation 131
- ◆ Cosmic Breathing Exercise 132
- ◆ Cleansing Your Body, Chakras and Your Auric Field 133
- ◆ How to Create Silver and Gold Pyramids of Protection 136
- ◆ Boogie Busting Process 138
- ◆ Earth Cleansing & Planetary Healing 140
- ◆ Closing Down, the Final Stage of Meditation 141
- ◆ House Cleaning and Protection 142

Meditation and Prayers

What is Meditation and Why Do You Need it?

Every day of our lives our mind is always active and it never stops. There is always an event or project on our minds or simply positive or negative daydreaming taking place within our minds. I can only compare the working of the mind to a freeway without traffic lights where each car is driving at the highest speed without any worry in the world. Up until now, you may not have had the need to install "traffic lights" inside your mind to stop your chaotic thoughts at will. But when you realize that in order to change your life for the better and actually step on the road to self-discovery, the first subject that will be introduced to you by your teachers is MEDITATION.

With regular Meditation, you will learn how to still the mind and to ignore the flow of thoughts, ideas and sounds. Meditation or chanting mantras is a very powerful mind exercise. Without it you cannot ensure spiritual self-awareness or communication with your spirit guides. Once you have decided to step on the journey of self-awareness, daily meditation **is not only optional but a must**. Meditation will serve as an agent for **balancing** your three levels of consciousness, **clearing and balancing all your chakras, clearing** and **strengthening your auric field** and thereby **preventing** any **negative beings** attaching themselves to you, or from influencing you in any manner. By the time you are ready to communicate with the higher guides, your auric field will be able to accommodate that process. In addition, your Lower Ego (the emotional body) will get the message that its leadership in your life is NO MORE, and gradually it has to learn to surrender itself to the Higher Ego (the Soul consciousness).

A Variety of Meditations to Choose From

- Guided Meditation,
- Chanting of Sacred Mantras
- and Prayer

At the beginning of your journey, it is highly recommended that you experiment with all of these three types of meditation to see which one works the best for you.

Guided meditation–This is when you listen to a voice-recorded meditation that will tell you a story which you need to follow mentally. At the beginning, your mind will interrupt you by allowing ideas and thoughts to come in. For instance: the thought that you have to pick up milk from the shop before you get home. When you become aware of this, just stop paying attention to those incoming thoughts and pick up the guided meditation wherever it is at that particular time. If you listen to this guided meditation every day, you will notice the interruptions will happen less and less with each subsequent day. Within seven to ten days, the interfering thoughts will stop altogether, and your meditation will progress in leaps and bounds.

Mantra repetition or Chanting (singing) is the process of repeating a mantra or positive affirmation either aloud or silently a number of times. It is optional, but the potency is stronger when a mantra is repeated 21 times, or 108 times.

In Sanskrit: the sound of AUM is the name of God.
AUM is the primeval sound that was caused by the vibration of creation. The entire universe is vibrant with the sound of AUM, (or as pronounced Ooom), which in Hinduism is known as the source of all mantras. Aum is considered to be the most fundamental and powerful mantra.

Om Namah Shivaya is known as the great redeeming mantra also known as the five-syllable mantra. It means "I bow to Shiva." Shiva is the supreme reality, the inner Self. It is the name given to the consciousness that dwells in all beings. Shiva is the name of your true identity–yourself. Om Namah Shivaya is a very powerful mantra. It can be repeated by anyone, young or old, rich or poor and no matter what state a person is in, it will purify them.

Om Mani Padme Hum

This mantra originated in India. As it moved from India into Tibet, Tibetan Buddhists believed that saying the mantra, ***Om Mani Padme Hum***, aloud or silently to oneself, invokes powerful benevolent attention and blessings in the embodiment of compassion.

Any prayers to God are also very powerful Mantras, which are used widely by anyone of any faith.

First Prayer.

Heavenly Father of the Universe.
In the name of my divine Christ light I now attune myself to my Divine Higher Self, to the Ascended Masters, and to the Divine Holy essence of Love, Light and Truth.

Second Prayer.

By Godfrey Ray King which can be found in the "I Am" Discourses.

Divine Father.
Take my love, and let it flow in fullness and devotion to thee.
Take my hands and let them work incessantly for thee.
Take my Soul and let it be merged in oneness with thee.
Take my mind and thoughts and let them be in tune with thee.
Take my everything, and let me be an instrument of thy work.

Third Prayer.
The Lord's Prayer

Our Father, Who art in Heaven Hallowed be Thy name.
Thy kingdom come, Thy will be done on Earth, as it is in Heaven. Give us this day our daily bread, and forgive us our trespasses, as we forgive those who trespass against us. Lead us not into temptation, but deliver us from evil, for Thine is the kingdom, the power and the glory.
AMEN

Fourth Prayer
This prayer was channeled by Dr Joshua Stone

I ask to be clothed in a robe of light, made of Divine Love, Wisdom and Compassion. Please protect me from any negative influences. Charge my auric field with the violet consuming flame of light, which consumes all negative vibrations. I do not accept any lesser guidance from the lower planes. The only guidance I accept is the Monadic and Logoic planes of the Ascended Masters. As you look up, the Divine Ascended masters hold towards you a robe made from the Divine Grace of love, light, truth, and compassion. See this robe placed around your shoulders. You feel as though the robe penetrates your mind, your body and even your spirit. Harmony and oneness with your divine self permeates through your heart to their heart. Anything you need to know, you only need to ask this Ascended Master and they will show you the answers you need for yourself or for another. The information will be presented to you in a vision, or through telepathic communication, which is conscious channeling.

Fifth Prayer.

The Great Invocation by Alice A. Bailey

From the point of Light within the Mind of God
Let light stream forth into the minds of men.
Let Light descend on Earth.
From the point of Love within the Heart of God
Let love stream forth into the hearts of men.
May Christ return to Earth.
From the centre where the Will of God is known
Let purpose guide the little wills of men–
The purpose which the Masters know and serve.
From the centre which we call the race of men
Let the Plan of Love and Light workout.
And may it seal the door where evil dwells.
Let Light and Love and Power restore the Plan on Earth.

And as a final option for meditation:

Selecting classical or new age music of your choice.

Within This Meditation

The contents of this particular meditation were channeled through me by the Ascended Masters many years ago when I was teaching self-awareness classes. The formatting of the meditation is very powerful, yet it is suitable for all levels of consciousness, regardless of whether the person is a beginner or more advanced. When this guided meditation is read out by anyone and recorded onto tape or CD, it should last only 50 to 55 minutes. Please never hesitate to make the recording for yourself. Or if you do not like listening to your own voice, ask someone you know whose voice you are happy to hear in the recording. One more word of advice on this subject, when you are ready to record, first select some nice new-age music and gently play it in the background. This way the meditation will be more powerful and much nicer to listen to.

How to Prepare Yourself for Meditation

1. **Selecting a Deity**. The first step you need to do is to select a Deity with whom you feel comfortable addressing yourself. The Deity you choose can be Buda, Jesus or one of the other Ascended Masters. If you do not feel comfortable at this stage because you cannot visualize or feel affinity to any of them, you may just visualize standing in front of the Sun, or a white/pink radiant light. This will represent the Higher Power that you feel most comfortable with.

2. **selecting a prayer** within the contents of this meditation a variety of prayers have been selected for you. Please select the one which you feel is most appropriate for you, or make up one of your own.

3. **Select some new age music**, light a white candle, and select a comfortable place to sit so you can begin your meditation.

Cosmic Breathing Exercise.

Any meditation you do **now** or in the **future** always starts with the cosmic breathing exercise. Your meditation will benefit from this type of breathing more than you can imagine. This breathing exercise is taught in Ancient Esoteric Science. For the pathway **of the cosmic force** to reach the Earth, you need to take one breath through the crown chakra (your head), and breathe out through the soles of your feet. For the pathway **of the earth energy** to reach the higher realms, you need to inhale through the soles of your feet chakra, and exhale through the crown chakra. You will need to repeat this breathing exercise three times. Always count when you are taking a breath from the crown chakra.

So let's begin.
First you must bring your conscious awareness to a place above your head.–You will notice that a radiant white beam of light is positioned 5 cm above your crown chakra.

Note: In reality you will still be breathing through your nose, you breathe through your chakras only in your imagination.

a) Take a deep breath and inhale that white beam of light **through your crown chakra**–and as you hold your breath, visualize the white light travelling down through each upper chakra until it reaches your heart chakra–and as you get ready to exhale–push the white light down into the chakras below until you reach the base chakra–the white light will now split into two beams– and each light path or beam will continue to flow through the left leg and the right leg–and then exit through the soles of your feet–and finally into the earth.

b) This time you will **breathe through the soles of your feet from the bottom of your body upwards towards your crown chakra**,–as you inhale, the radiant light will travel up through your legs–as the light enters into the base chakra and then travels upwards through the chakras–then it enters into your heart chakra–and as you get ready to exhale–you push the light upwards through the upper chakras–and finally upwards through to the crown chakra.

Then begin breathing through the top chakra again as in the first exercise above (b), until you have completed the three sets of inhalations. After this breathing exercise you can continue with the meditation below.

Cleansing Your Body, Chakras and Your Auric field

Imagine and visualize far above your head, (about 60 meters) a radiating golden orb of light appearing–which resembles a miniature Sun.–This golden orb represents your Divine God consciousness–which in reality is your Higher Self.

From the golden orb of light–a silvery white stream of light descends towards you–and begins to enfold your entire body–this silvery white light extends about 5 meters below your feet–below your Earth chakra–it then begins to manifest itself into a silver dish below your feet–the silver dish is about 3 meters in diameter and it expands all around you–and below your feet–as you look down–you notice that beneath the soles of your feet–a small silver disc is holding your entire body suspended above the silver dish of light–the silvery white light begins to penetrate through your skin–permeating through every cell of your body–then the light begins to remove and dislodge the dark residue from each cell of your body–and pushes this dark energy towards the surface of your skin–the dark energy represents all the negative and painful memories–which you have accumulated within your four body systems–in a short space of time your entire body will be covered with dark soot–which is composed of negative emotional energies that you have created in the past, and just recently.

From the golden orb, more silver light emanates towards you–which feels like a summer shower and begins to wash all this dark energy from the surface of your skin–the silver light removes the residue easily and effortlessly–and begins to slide down below your feet into the silver dish.

Move your conscious awareness to your head and shoulder region–as they begin to feel–cleansed and free of residue–as the silver light works itself down your body–cleaning and brushing down your chest area–moving towards your waistline–the light keeps moving further down your body–and you begin to feel lighter and lighter. The light continues to move down your legs–passing below your knees–and down to your feet–suddenly a tingling sensation runs throughout your entire body–you are beginning to feel lighter with each passing second–and free of the negative residue.

A rod of silvery white light is now descending–and entering through your crown chakra–and it begins to travel down until it reaches the base of your spine–as it is passing through each chakra–it will open them up–at the front and also at the back of your body–as each chakra begins to open up simultaneously–each one begins to resemble a small floodgate–and pushes all the dark emotional residues out–the dark sludge is pouring out and flows directly into the silver dish beneath your feet–please bring your attention back–to your **crown chakra**–you will notice that all the darkness has flown out–and from the center of the chakra a new light begins to emerge–many colors within the light begin to resemble all the colors of the rainbow–these colors are harmonizing–healing and balancing your crown chakra on all levels of your being. **Now please look down to your next chakra below.**

Your Third Eye chakra just finished with the cleansing–and slowly the colors of the rainbow are manifesting through the center–and installing healing–spiritual clarity and understanding–harmony and balance on all levels of your being. **Now, please look down to your next chakra below.**

Your Heart chakra–has also been emptied of darkness–and slowly at first–the colors of the rainbow manifest through–and install healing–love for self and others–harmony and balance on all levels of your being.
Now, please look down to your next chakra below.

Your Solar plexus–has also been emptied of darkness–and slowly at first–the colors of the rainbow manifest through–and install healing–clarity and understanding and oneness with the world and beyond–harmony and balance on all levels of your being. **Now, please look down to your next chakra below.**

Your Emotional chakra–just emptied itself of darkness–and slowly at first–the colors of the rainbow begin to manifest through–and install healing–self-respect for self and others–harmony and balance on all levels of your being. **Now please look down to your next chakra below.**

And finally your Base chakra–has also been emptied of darkness–and slowly at first–the colors of the rainbow begin to manifest through–and install healing–wellbeing–harmony and balance on all levels of your being–all the back chakras have also finished clearing and balancing at the same time as the front chakras–a tingling sensation begins to run through your entire being,–you feel balanced–harmonized on all levels of your being. **Look down** below your feet–and you will see that the silver dish is filled up to the brim with the dark residue.

From the golden orb above you, a golden disc descends down towards you–and passes down through your entire body–as it moves down–it leaves golden strands of light within your aura and through your body–this golden light harmonizes and balances you, on all levels of your being. **As the golden disc** continues to descend below your feet–and when it reaches the silver dish–it stops right above it–and then sets itself like a lid on top of the dish–and seals the dish down.
Two Angelic beings then appear in front of you–and remove this dish from beneath your feet–They then fly away toward the Sun. –As they move closer to the Sun–they become smaller and smaller. As they reach the Sun, they throw the dish into the Sun–to burn and transform the negative energy into an unconditional healing love of light. Next, ask the Divine Love of light to send this transformed light to the people from the past, with which you have co-created those negative energies.–You ask them to accept this blessing of love and healing, and remind them–that it was only a lesson that was not fully understood at the time.

How to Create Silver and Gold Pyramids of Protection

a) From the golden orb of light–a white beam of light begins to descend down towards you–It enters through the top of your head–(*your crown chakra*)–and begins to move down through your spine–as it is passing through each and every chakra–below your feet–and down into your Earth chakra–the light continues to pass through until it anchors itself into the center of the Earth.–Your spinal column is radiating with this white beam of light.– **Next**, expand this beam of light throughout your body–keep expanding the light out–until it reaches the walls of the room–in which you are sitting right now.– **Then**, visualize the light transforming itself into a four-sided pyramid–which completely encases the room–As you look down onto the floor of the room–from wall to wall, a carpet of white light stretches and covers the entire floor–and the light continues to penetrate deep down, into the Earth.

b) Now, from the golden orb, a golden beam of light begins to descend down towards you–it enters through the top of your head–it flows down through your spine–and below your feet–until it reaches the center of the Earth.–**Now**, expand this golden beam of light throughout your body–and out into the room until it reaches 10 cm away from the white pyramid walls–**Now begin** creating a second pyramid with the golden light.–**As you** look down onto the floor of the room–from wall to wall–a carpet of golden light stretches and covers the entire floor–So, now the room is encased by two pyramids–the first pyramid is silvery white–which keeps out all the invading negative energies and beings–and the second is a gold pyramid which gives you and your household–harmony and wellbeing within mind–body–and spirit.

c)–The third time, from the golden orb above your head, **an icy pink** beam of light descends down towards you–enters through the top of your head–passes through your crown chakra–and then flows down through your spine all the way to below your feet–**Expand** this icy pink light all around you–and then fill up the room with it. **Take a deep breath**–as you inhale this icy pink light–you begin to feel as if your mind body-spirit is transforming and realigning itself with the divine healing of love and light and truth–on all levels of your being.

Establishing a Communication Channel From the Present Personality, to your Higher Self, And to the Ascended Masters.

Connection to the Sun

This part of the meditation is recommended to those who are ready to channel the spiritual Hierarchy from the higher realms, and specially recommended for those who are about to become a professional spiritual healer or a tarot or palm reader for the public.

I would like you to move your conscious awareness to your heart chakra. Within the center of your heart, a golden spiral of light emerges, and begins spiraling upwards.–It penetrates through your throat chakra,–then through the third eye chakra,–up through the crown chakra,–until it reaches the golden orb of light above your head.–The golden spiral of light penetrates and travels through the golden orb–and then spirals up towards the Sun in our Solar system. The golden spiral of light enters into the Sun,–within the Sun, three "beams of light" are emerging and they are gold–white gold–and pink.–They begin to entwine with one another, to form a rope.–This rope represents "the divine connection to the Hierarchy". The three-colored rope then intertwines with your golden spiral, and they become one with each other and form a divine connection.–The rope begins to descend towards your golden orb–"your Higher-Self connection"–pierces through it, and keeps traveling towards your physical body.–The rope then continues and penetrates through your Crown charka.–Third Eye chakra,–Throat chakra,–Heart chakra,–Solar plexus chakra,–Naval chakra,–Base chakra–and then into your Earth chakra.

Take a deep breath,–you realize you are breathing in an icy pink light.–You begin to feel peace and harmony and pure unconditional love enter your mind, body and spirit.–You feel in harmony with the Divine Supreme God of love and light, and truth and compassion. **Take another deep breath**–and this time you are inhaling blue and gold light–which expands your Spiritual awareness of yourself and brings in harmony and balance with the Divine Christ of love and light. **As you take the third deep**

breath–you begin to inhale a beautiful purple and green color of light.–You then feel harmony and wellbeing expand throughout your body, on all levels of your being.

At this point in time you notice one of the Ascended Masters appear in front of you. Kneel before this presence and state your purpose and request.

Boogie Busting Process

Visualize yourself standing in a green meadow–surrounded by snow-capped mountains.–As you turn around towards your left side, a few meters away, a gateway will appear.–This gateway is connected and leads up to the higher astral planes.–This is where the departed or lost Souls usually arrive first.–As you will see, next to the gate, there is a control panel.–You only need to place your left hand on the panel to activate it, and as you do so, the tunnel lights up with the most brilliant colors that radiate out and fill up the whole valley.– **From the tunnel**, Angelic beings come out to aid and assist the transition.–These Angels are called **the Karmic Council force of police escorts**. They assemble themselves forming a big circle from the left side of the gateway, to the right side of the gate. **You** find yourself standing in the center of the circle.–To assist you in your task, four archangels will appear within the circle, near you.–The first Archangel Raphael, with his blue sword to cut the cord.–Then Archangel Michael,–Archangel Gabriel, and Archangel Uriel.

A large oval mirror will appear in front of you. This mirror is magical because when you look into this mirror–you will see yourself like never before.–You may see dark cords hanging and dangling from different parts of your body–and in some places more than others–but mostly they are around some of your chakra regions.–The Archangels are here to supervise the situation, and you feel comfortable with the process that is about to take place. **Suddenly you feel compelled to touch one of the cords**–as you do so, the cord immediately detaches from your body–and as you hold this in your hand, you will see for the very first time–that at the end of the cord there is a shadowy figure attached to it–this shadowy figure is a lost soul, who attached itself to you some time ago.

One of the Archangels will be standing right next to you–and will take the cord out of your hand. Once the angel gets a hold of that dark cord, they will begin to walk through the star gate,–to escort the lost soul to their destined place within the astral plane.

Please do not attempt to speak with the departing Soul. You do not need to know the reason why they have attached themselves to you in the first place. **One after the other**, pull those cords away from your body. Don't just let it go–hand it over to the Karmic angel next to you and they will take that cord from you, and walk with that lost Soul through the star gate–Begin pulling out each and every one of those cords–until the front of your body is free of attachments–It is time to pay attention to the back of your body.–You can view this easily, because you realize that a big magic mirror stands right behind you.–This time the Karmic Angels will step in and within a minute they pull out all the remaining attachments–and the angels will walk them through the star gate.

For the first time, you are free of all the attachments, and you begin to feel lighter than ever before.–**From the golden orb** of light above you–a light of rainbow colors descends towards you–transforming itself into a robe–and settling down around your shoulders–The robe covers you from head to toe.–The robe will give you divine protection at all times. When you finish the clearing process, turn towards the Karmic Angels, and the Archangels, and give thanks for their guidance and supervision. **Then** they will begin to walk through the star gate, and when the last being has walked through–then you walk up to the panel and place the right palm of your hand on the surface.–This action will close the star gate down.

Now–I would like you to start spinning like a ballerina, towards the right side of your body, and begin to spin faster and faster–this motion transports you back to your physical reality, or any time you wish to change dimensions of reality–Now you begin to slow down, until you come to a standstill.

Earth Cleansing & Planetary Healing

You may continue on with this part when you are finished with the "boogie busting" or towards the end of Meditation, or simply just use this on its own at a different time.

Visualize taking a giant Leap up into the air and finding to your amazement that you can fly.–As you keep rising away from the ground, high up into the atmosphere–within a short space of time you realize that you reach the outer region of the earth's ozone layer, you slow down and stop at a comfortable distance–until Planet Earth is well below you. Suddenly you realize that you are not alone–from out of nowhere the cosmos is filled with a variety of Angels and Spirit guides–They welcome you–and are happy to assist you to heal the Earth and its four kingdoms.

Ask permission from Mother Earth to accept healing from you for cleansing her.–From the golden orb above you, a beam of white light descends towards you.–It enters through your crown chakra and into your heart chakra.–As you open up your heart center a silvery white beam of light pours out.–You take up position right above the north pole where the spine of the earth begins–and direct the light beam from your heart chakra into the North Pole,–the light will travel through the earth's spine, which will come out at the South Pole–As the silver beam of light fills up the earth's spinal column,–the light begins to expand throughout the Planet,–until it reaches beyond the ozone layer.

The silvery white light filters, pushes and carries with it all negative residues–and pushes this up just beyond the ozone layer.–You will also notice that certain parts of the Planet are covered with dark clouds.–If you look into your right hand, you will find that a big butterfly net has just appeared.–This is a magical net–and your inner knowing is telling you to scoop up the dark clouds with your net.–As you are flying above one of those dark clouds, and scoop some up with your butterfly net,–suddenly you realize from the end of your net a white/pink light is pouring out,–and the pink light is falling back onto the Earth.–This can only mean one thing–that you are carrying a magical net in your hand, which can transform dark negative energy into pink loving light. –**Now**, with this realization and magic device, you then begin to fly around the earth and start to gather up all those dark clouds–and transform them all into pink clouds of light.–Within a short period of time you see that half of the Planet is already blanketed under -the pink light.–With a fast circle around the Planet and a final scoop up,–the entire Planet is covered with pink light.–Now you are ready to deliver the last stage of healing. Positioning yourself once again above the North Pole,–from your heart chakra direct the colors of the rainbow into the spine of the Earth.–See that it expands throughout the Planet. It is radiating with divine healing. This spectrum of light will transform every cell within the four kingdoms,–and install divine love, wisdom and harmony.–Your heart chakra stops emanating the light.–You have done what you have set out to do, and suddenly realize you are gently drawn back to planet Earth.–As you enter the atmosphere,–flying through the white clouds–you find that you move closer and closer to a green meadow. –As you reach the ground, and stand firmly on the ground, you are immediately ready to spin towards the right side of your body.–**As you begin to spin**, first fast then in a short space of time–you begin to slow down gradually to a standstill.

Closing down, the final stage of Meditation

Take a deep breath, and as you slowly exhale–you begin to feel sensations in your body and realize that you are seated in a chair,–or lying on the floor. **Take another deep breath**, and as you exhale, you begin to be aware of–your face–your shoulders–your chest–your legs and your whole body all the way down to your toes. **Take another deep breath**, and as you exhale, open your eyes, and be fully awake and alert to start your day.

House Cleaning and Protection.

This meditation can be part of the long meditation or it can be used on its own independently.

Now picture yourself in front of your house, on the footpath once more.–The Sun is high in the sky, right above your house. **From the Sun a silvery white beam of light descends** and penetrates through the center of your home,–approximately 800 meters below ground level.–The silvery light then begins to expand and fill the outer boundaries of your property and transforms itself into a big silver pyramid above your property encasing your house and garden within.–The pyramid then expands to about 100 meters above your house. **Now look down** onto the ground, and see a carpet of silver white light that stretches from boundary to boundary across your property,–sinking into the Earth below your home–approximately 800 meters.

From the Sun a golden beam of light descends, entering through the silver tip of the pyramid–down through the house and into the Earth to reach the 800-metre mark. **It then expands through** the house into the garden–until it reaches the silver white pyramid wall, stopping 10 cm short,–then taking up the shape of a golden pyramid. **When you look down** onto the ground, a carpet of golden light overlays the other carpet of light,–and sinks about 700 meters into the ground.

From the Sun, a rainbow color of light descends entering through the tip of the silver and golden pyramids filling the garden and the inside of the house.–This energy brings with it love– light and harmony–and protection to fill your home inside and out.

From your front gate, through your front door to your back door,–the Karmic Angels begin to install a silver tunnel of light.–Any visitor or family member may bring a lost Soul or negative thought-form into your house.–This tunnel will instantly transform the energy of any lost Souls or thought-form who may follow any members of your family or a visiting friend who comes into your house.–The Karmic Angels will transport them all instantly to their proper destination.

This house cleaning and protection exercise should be repeated every day for the next 6 weeks. After that, once or twice a week should be sufficient. Your household will stay clear at all times.

If You Are Living in a High Rise Building between Two Floors

Visualize yourself, being able to stand in the air, as if you would be standing on solid ground.–Instead of creating a pyramid to encase your household,–create a wall of light below and above the floors, which will encase your flat in a silver box,–this will separate your household from the other tenants. It will work, without any problems.

In regards to Boogie Busting–After you have cleansed yourself *and you wish to clean a family member, simply visualize that person right in front of you to clear the dark cord attachments from him/her. You no longer need the mirrors. They disappear from the circle as soon as you have finished cleaning yourself. Start by pulling the cords off the person, one by one, and handing them over to the Karmic Angels. When the person is clean, visualize all the colors of the rainbow descending down towards them from their golden orb of light and then assembling into a robe of light, which will cover them from top to bottom. When you find yourself stronger and better at this process, you can do more than one person.*

10th
CHAPTER

CONTENTS

◆ Crystals to Aid and Protect You **146**

◆ How to Clear Your Crystals **147**

◆ How to Program Each Crystal **147**

◆ The Spiritual Light Worker's Etiquette **149**

◆ Closing **153**

Crystals to Aid and Protect You

The human body is energetic in nature and responds well to crystals. Crystals have been used from the beginning of time and can assist us by promoting harmony as well as to help to align human energies by balancing the chakra system of the body. Quartz crystals are excellent when programmed for healing, meditation and channeling, and anything you would need to enhance your energy. Special crystals are used as a gateway to the inner Self and as a connection to the Higher Self. A one-inch (about 2 ½ cm,) crystal has about 1 to 1 ½ meters energy expansion.

In order to aid you on your journey, I highly recommend you use crystals, and if you are a spiritual worker, keep some crystals nearby, and also you can wear them as jewellery. It is not a must, if for some reason you do not want them, it will be OK not to have them around you. This does not mean you will get less information when you are doing any spiritual work.

For more information on crystals I highly recommend the book:
By Melody–"Love *is in the Earth –A Kaleidoscope of Crystals*''.

Combinations of Certain Crystals, and Higher Vibrations

It is normal that some crystals will appeal to you more than others. When you use two crystals together, their energy consciousness is combined and will create a higher vibration.

Recommended combinations of crystals:

Amethyst with Green Fluorite–Helps to clean out characteristics from our Subconscious mind, such as the negative re-acquiring belief systems and tendencies, which are no longer needed.

Any green and blue colour crystals–Together they help to bring out the full spiritual potential of your Soul consciousness, and the realization and identification of the God within.

- **Gold**–assists with inner realization and Christ consciousness.
- **Silver**–assists with purification of Mind–Body–and Spirit.
- **White Pearls**–and rose quartz together brings in Divine Love and Wisdom.

How to Clear your Crystals

Your crystals need to be cleansed and recharged, especially if other people handle them or if you use them for healing. Three days before a Full or New Moon, bury the crystals in the ground, about 10-20 cm into the earth and cover them over with soil. I recommend that you first put your crystals in a net, so that when you are ready to dig them up, they can easily be found. They do have a tendency to disappear, especially when they are small pieces.

Leave them in the ground for seven days altogether. Then rinse them under a tap and place the crystals where the morning Sun will shine on them as it rises. Let the Sun shine on the crystals for no more than two hours. With this clearing ritual, your crystals will be re-energized by the Earth's magnetic field, the Sunlight, and the lunar energies. Now you have very powerful crystals to use, and re-program if you wish to do so. You need to repeat this cleansing process every three to six months.

How to Program Each Crystal.

The best crystal to program is the Quartz crystal, especially when used for meditation, or as a healing tool etc. However, any crystals can be programmed in the same manner as above.

Hold the crystal between your thumb and your index finger using both of your hands. Hold the crystal in front of your third eye and project a thought form, whatever you may wish the crystal to do for you.

For example, you could say: Crystal, I program you to aid me with your energy of consciousness and Divine Wisdom, to give me protection from any invading negative influence or interference, and transform the negative energies and thought forms into healing loving light. **Then**, visualize your chosen Ascended Master, or any of the Archangels appearing in front of you, as you hand over your crystal to that being.

(In the physical reality, you just lower the crystal away from your third eye and cradle it in the palm of your hands, and offer it up to the Master or the Angel to be blessed.)

The Ascended Master will take it out of your hands and radiate the blessing of energy into it, and put it back into your palms again.

After the blessing, do not **allow** anyone, except you, to handle your programmed crystal, because their energy will interfere with the programming. If they touch your crystal accidentally, or without being aware that it was programmed, there is no need to panic. Place the crystal on an amethyst cluster, and that will clear out the foreign energy. After two to three hours, you will have to re-program your crystal again.

The Spiritual Light Worker's Etiquette

Please Never Forget That Firstly ***EVERYONE*** *is a Soul Consciousness*

Being a professional Tarot and Palm reader myself, I have written a textbook on Tarot cards, the title of which is, "*How to Channel from the Akashic Records When You Are Reading Tarot Cards*"
In this tarot card book, I have also included the very much needed guidelines of Etiquette for those who may be considering becoming a spiritual light worker within the profession of healing, a tarot reader or in the field of many specialties. I have devised these guidelines from a professional tarot and palm reader's point of view. But these guidelines can be applied to any field and I hope that you may find them useful in your journey. When you are in a position to give a reading or any form of spiritual service to a client, please keep in mind that just because they are unable to remember their own Divinity, and they identify mostly with their Physical and Emotional body at this stage; that does not mean that their inner Soul Guidance is not actively monitoring what is going on. There is a warning bell about to ring anytime to warn the client if lies and a false story are about to be told. If you or anyone else is doing a "reading" and you begin to make up stories as you go along, in other words, you are lying through your teeth, everyone will pick that up. Never underestimate anyone's intelligence or intuition!

For example: if you are the client, and someone else is reading your cards, the first thing you will feel is a funny, uncomfortable feeling beginning to stir within your solar plexus. It will warn you that something is not right. If you listen to the warning, the reader also gets the message that the lying is not working any more, and then the story is not going anywhere or making sense any longer. Then the usual things will take place; you will complain and demand your money back, or leave very dissatisfied. When people have a variety of readers to choose from, like at the Mind, Body, Spirit festival, (Australia) or at any organized Spiritual Fair, they have the chance to see the readers, and feel some affinity towards one of them. It is like your inner knowing will recognize the correct reader and it then lets you know that this is the right one for you. Usually, that reader will be able to answer most of your questions and give you the message that you are ready for and need to know, this time around. Then the reader will have a happy client, and a very good reading.

When the right client seeks you out for a reading that is because they are drawn to you as the Reader. Then you will always have a successful reading. **When the client** seeks you out for a reading because of a friend's recommendation, or someone that they know who was very impressed by all the things that you predicted, it could be a very different matter. This person never had the slightest inclination to have any type of a reading, but they have a few problems and a few questions, and would not mind knowing something more. Therefore, they make a booking with you, and expect you to make all their problems **disappear instantly**. You find that within a short time during the reading, you lose them. It feels like you are speaking to them in a foreign language, and they are ready to argue about what you are saying and forecasting. They have not realized that the prediction is about to be played out in the future. But according to them, it **cannot and will not happen**, as you just said it would. In this case, you are reading their cards correctly, but not at their level of comprehension. They are not ready to hear the truth about themselves at this point in time. They need a different reader who will be able to speak at their level of understanding.

For Example: The "wrong" client seeks me out, and I begin to read their palms, which carry their blueprint. The blueprint is based upon their past lives and present life possibilities for their journey in this lifetime. I also see why they are here on this Earth, which Galaxy they have originated from and what shape, form and strength may be in their Mental, Emotional and Spiritual bodies at this moment in time. The client, who has not been exposed to Spiritual self-discovery yet, will find this information very strange, and it will sound like a science fiction story. They will not be able to understand what I am talking about. At this stage, I know how to read to their level of understanding, but it is energetically very difficult and taxing on me to do so. The only way I can describe this for you is to ask you to imagine yourself in a ten-storey apartment building. You work and live on the tenth floor, but someone on the first floor decides to ask your opinion about something very important to them. They cannot go up to the tenth floor, and you are not allowed to go down to their floor either. Therefore, you both stand out in the hallway, and start talking to one another by leaning over the rails on your balconies. Your voices will be tuned to a certain volume. Hearing and understanding will be very difficult between the two of you. The person on the first floor will be very unhappy with the results. Let us continue using the ten-storey apartment building as an example. We will use this analogy as a level of consciousness in progress. Each floor contains a certain degree of wisdom to be gained by each individual, and each floor contains the **correct teachers** (those who will give you a hard time, or guide you with wisdom and love; they will usually be your parents, relatives, friends, neighbors, workmates, spouse, etc.) to aid you, and everyone else on their journey.

Each floor will also have the right people who will have the ability to read your blueprint, to tell you where you are now, where you need to go next to achieve or change your life for the better. These types of people are the professional Tarot card readers, Palm readers, Astrologers, Numerologists, Healers, and so forth. When you go to the wrong floor, (the one you have not yet reached, or the one that you do not belong to any longer,) the information about you will be distorted and incomprehensible. You will subsequently be confused and unhappy with the outcome of the reading. Your inner guidance will always warn you in advance. What you need to do is listen to it. If you are looking for someone to read for you, please ask your divine guidance to lead you to the right Reader, who can read for you at your level of understanding. You will find it amazing that when you ask to be guided to the right reader, it will actually work! Otherwise, you will blame the reader and call the person a charlatan and many other names. You are to blame in the first place since you ignored the warnings of your inner guidance.

For you as the reader it is very important to request from the Ascended Masters in your meditation to only send you the right type of people for readings, and that they are on your level of ability. Also it is important that they can understand, and are ready for, the information to be received through you about themselves. With the right information given to the client, you have provided a very important service to humanity, and to that client. Because of that information, the client will have more clarity and will be able to change their life for the better.

Cause and Effect means: Whatever you give out comes back like a boomerang. In Sanskrit, this is called "***Karma***"

This Law applies throughout your journey of life. When you harm or want to hurt someone, even to the smallest degree, you will suffer the same consequences. If you have done this without meaning to, you will receive it back only single fold. If you do the harm knowingly, you will receive it back twofold.

The first fold of punishment is because you knowingly went out of your way to hurt someone.

Second fold, whatever your victim suffered you will also suffer in the same way, or to that degree. This is called double the **Karma**.

For example: Let's say that when a reader has not bothered to learn the rules and principles of the Tarot, they possibly work from their Lower Ego, (channeling the Lost Souls and negative entities) then the reader is abusing their power. They tell stories to the client that are not true, causing them to be fearful of their loved ones. To add to this, the reader charges the client "highway robbery" prices!

Closing

We have come to the end of our journey. As you have been introduced to the science of the mind/body/spirit you realize, after you have attained this knowledge, that you no longer have any excuse to fall back on as to why you cannot make better choices in every situation you are going to face within the near future.

One last word of advice, please don't be too hard on yourself. Be patient, and just take one step at a time, because eventually you will be able to train your Lower Ego to listen and learn and surrender to the High Egos guidance. Remember practice will make you perfect.

With Love & Light & Truth
Rozália

***

Rozália would like to receive your feedback on the contents of this book. **In addition**, if you like the contents of the book I would like to make a request: please let your friends or other like-minded people know about its availability.

How to order the book of; "*How to Channel from the Akashic Records When You Are Reading Tarot Cards*"

This book can be ordered from Amazon.com USA.
Or from the author within Australia please refer to my **Website**, and check out specials discounts, and download free sample chapters on my books.

If you wish to contact the author:
Ph: +61 2 9521 3951
Email: rozalia1@optusnet.com.au
Web: www.akashicrecords-tarot.com

www.ingramcontent.com/pod-product-compliance
Lightning Source LLC
Chambersburg PA
CBHW060930040426
42445CB00011B/874
9780646545141